Roman Egyptomania

Sally-Ann Ashton

With contributions from Ted Buttrey and Adrian Popescu

A Special exhibition at The Fitzwilliam Museum, Cambridge

24 September 2004 – 8 May 2005

Golden House Publications

Notes on the text

The directions within the catalogue entries are according to usual practice, unless stated otherwise. Coins are described from the viewer's perspective, but all other catalogue entries are described as if from the object's point of view according to proper left and right.

A basic reference is provided for each catalogue entry and includes publication, if relevant, with comparisons and further reading. The bibliography at the back of the book contains additional works that are relevant to the subject of this catalogue or might prove useful to the reader.

Contributors

Ted Buttrey provided the essay on coinage in Roman Egypt.

Adrian Popescu wrote the basic entries for the coins, which were then adapted for the reader. I take full responsibility for any errors or interpretations here.

Nigel Cassidy is responsible for the photography of the following entries: 4, 5, 6, 8, II, 19, 26, 29, 30, 31, 32, 36, 39, 40, 44-46, 47-49, 53, 57, 58, 59, 60, 65-67, 69-70, 71, 72-74, 75, 76-77, 78, 80, 81, 82, 83, 84, 85, 86, 87, 88, 89, 90, 91, 92, 94, 95, 96, 97, 98, 99, 107, 109.

Andrew Morris and Andrew Norman are responsible for the photography of the following entries: 7, 12, 79, 93, 102, 103, 108 and figure 1.

Evangeline Markou is responsible for producing the images for the following entries: 1, 2, 3, 9, 10, 13, 14, 15, 16, 17, 18, 20, 21, 22, 23, 24, 25, 27, 28, 33, 34, 35, 37, 38, 41, 42, 43, 50, 51, 52, 54, 55, 56, 61, 62, 63, 64, 100, 101.

Printed in the United Kingdom
by Panther, Print & Design Ltd
7 Trafalgar Business Centre
77 River Road
Barking
Essex IGII 0JU
020 8591 1005

Golden House Publications
PO Box 4919
London WIA IGH
United Kingdom
GoldenHouse@aol.com

ISBN 0-9547218-5-3

Acknowledgements

I would like to thank Lucilla Burn and Helen Strudwick for their comments on the text and for offering advice on arrangement and also additional bibliography. I would also like to thank Julie Dawson for her input on the condition and peculiarities of many of the objects in this exhibition, it was great fun trying to work out how many pieces had been manufactured and the text contains many of Julie's thoughts. All three have offered great encouragement for which I am especially grateful. I would also like to thank Stephen Quirke for his help.

I would like to thank Julia Poole of the Department of Applied Arts for her advice on and willingness to include the Osiris-Antinous statues. In the Department of Coins and Medals Adrian Popescu provided the basic entries for the coins that are included in this catalogue and Ted Buttrey wrote the essay on coins in Roman Egypt and offered further advice on the entries. Evangeline Markou patiently scanned all of the coins that are illustrated in this catalogue and worked wonders with some very difficult images.

I am grateful to Andrew Bednarski and Sarah Parcak for their work at the Museum during this project. Both have been a great help in the final selection of objects and in planning the exhibition.

I would like to thank Cary Martin and John Tait for their comments on catalogue number 84. Judith Bunbury for helping with the identification of the hard-stones. I also wish to thank Michelle Lovric for her references on Justine Wynne.

I am extremely grateful to Nigel Cassidy for his enthusiasm, patience and skill in producing many new images for the catalogue, and Andrew Morris and Andrew Norman of the Photographic Department at the Fitzwilliam Museum have both offered further encouragement and support for the project.

I would like to thank Wolfram Grajetzki of Golden House Publications for his support and patience throughout the publication process and for his comments on number 84.

Finally, I would like to thank the Tomasso Brothers for sponsoring this catalogue and for their generous loan of three objects for the exhibition. Their enthusiasm has been a great encouragement throughout the project.

The theme of this exhibition is a result of a conversation that I had with, the now late, Sarah Clackson in Spring 2003. I am extremely grateful to Sarah for sharing her thoughts and ideas, and wish to acknowledge her encouragement for the project.

Sally-Ann Ashton
Cambridge 2004

Pyramid of Gaius Cestius, Rome

Introduction

Our knowledge of Romano-Egyptian culture derives from two different sources: sanctuaries and houses in Italy and Egyptian material that was manufactured during the Roman occupation of the province. There is a fundamental difference between the two categories, representing on the one hand an often misguided attempt to understand an alien culture- in Rome- and on the other a development of an established tradition in Egypt. It is important to understand this division and also to recognise the respective differences of the two cultures and how Egyptian art and culture developed in such diverse environments. There are many points of meeting between the two but the essential distinction is the audience. The consequence of this dual development was a form of material culture so novel that many of its products have been categorised as modern forgeries. In the case of the Egyptian-style objects found in Italy we find an attempt to copy and also to interpret material from another culture. The end result is an interesting blending of traditions and arguably the first instance of Egyptomania. Many of the objects are copies of originals and in some instances were intended to fool the viewer into believing that the object was an exotic import; we therefore encounter 'forgeries' - but they are Roman in date.

Like many museums, the Fitzwilliam houses a large collection of Romano-Egyptian material predominantly from excavations in Egypt, but it is also fortunate to have a number of exceptional pieces from Italy. The section of this catalogue on Egyptian culture in Rome is enhanced by the generous loan of two hard stone statues and a porphyry funerary urn from the Tomasso Brothers' private collection. The Fitzwilliam Museum also houses many objects from every-day life often preserved in settlements or funerary contexts in Egypt. However, the focus of this current exhibition and catalogue is the problem of interpreting of Romano-Egyptian culture, by both Romans and Egyptians. It also explores the validity of applying such cultural boundaries.

Section 1 considers the role of the emperors as pharaohs (a term used here to indicate their position as king of Egypt and a title which they often took), sections 2 and 3 explore how the Roman occupation of Egypt affected the native material culture. The final section of the exhibition considers objects from Italy that are inspired by Rome's contact with Egypt. The different culture of the audience, and the artists who produced this material, mean that it differs considerably from that found in Egypt. Interestingly, however, many changes to the appearance of recognised Egyptian gods were made by artists in Italy and then exported to their native Egypt. The Romans in Italy were in a similar position to Egyptophiles of the eighteenth and nineteenth centuries and as a consequence artists produced material, which was Egyptianising, inspired by Egypt but not necessarily comprehensible to Egyptians.

There have been several recent special exhibitions on aspects of Roman Egypt but few have attempted to look comprehensibly at the question of interaction between Egyptian and Roman art and material culture. Although this present catalogue is limited for the most part to objects from a single museum's collections, it aims to look specifically at the acculturation of the two traditions and cultures and to offer an introduction to what was arguably the earliest example of mass Egyptomania.

A marble bust of Marcus Aurelius, said to be from Alexandria,
The Fitzwilliam Museum Cambridge

Contents

Emperors and Pharaohs

During the late Ptolemaic period, Rome had enjoyed an increasing amount of power over Egypt, and finally in 30 BC, following the death of Cleopatra VII, absolute control. The first Roman to visit the country in his new capacity of pharaoh was Octavian, not an emperor until 27 BC when he became Augustus. As Augustus, he used the province as a means of self-promotion both at home and in Egypt itself, appearing on a vast number of native temples and bringing reminders of his victory to Rome. In the *Res Gestae*, a celebration of Augustus' achievements, the emperor wrote: 'I added Egypt to the empire of the Roman people' (*Res Gestae* 27). This was not, however, strictly accurate in that Egypt remained under the control of the emperor. Egypt enjoyed a special position and was different from other Roman provinces in that it was not directly governed by the Roman Senate. Instead, Egypt was directly under the control of the emperor and in his absence a Prefect, who was a Roman of the Equestrian rank, and so a man of considerable wealth. Other leading Equestrians and Senators were not permitted to enter the country without the permission of the emperor. This was a wise decision, given the tumultuous nature of many groups of the population, in particular the Alexandrians, who would fight each other or the authorities at a drop of a hat, or in one instance the price of a pair of shoes.

Ancient historians comment of Augustus' dislike of Egyptian religion, when asked if he would like to see the Apis bull at Memphis the ruler declined stating that he was 'accustomed to worshipping gods not cattle' (Dio Cassius 51.16.5). His use of Egyptian culture back in Rome seems purely to have been in order to promote his victory over Mark Antony and Cleopatra VII. However, on paper he was a model pharaoh, being amongst the most prolific of temple builders. Arnold (1999: 230-48) lists the building projects of Augustus to include: finishing the Temple to the Deified Julius Caesar in Alexandria, building a birth house of Isis-Hathor at Denderah, and another Temple of Isis at El'Qal'a near Koptos, where he also decorated the outer wall of the Geb shrine. Temples were also built at Shanhour in Upper Egypt and Deir el-Shelouit at Thebes. The Temple of Kom Ombo was enlarged, the forecourt of the Khnum Temple on Elephantine Island was finished and added to, and a large kiosk was built close to the entrance of the Temple of Isis on the Island of Philae; the entrance was also developed and the emperor's names and image decorate the gateway of Ptolemy II, alongside those of the early Ptolemaic ruler. A pylon was built at the Temple of Osiris on the Island of Biggeh, The Temple of Isis at Daboud was expanded, a kiosk was built at Qertassi, south of Philae and several projects were carried out at Kalabsha. Even the Western Desert was included in Augustus' building schemes. Temples were built at 'Ain Amur between Kharga and Dakhleh Oases, and it seems that an enclosure wall and gateway were added to the Temple of Amun the Victor at Dakhleh. In this way the arrival of the new pharaoh was celebrated and the ruler cult continued. The Egyptian priests must have been content that they had a king to fulfil the necessary roles. However, under the Romans the priesthood lost a considerable amount of their power (Thompson 1988: 272).

Later emperors clearly felt a more deferential link with Egypt than Augustus. Temples continued to be built showing the absent pharaohs in the traditional guise of king performing well-established ceremonies throughout the land. The new exotic cults were also promoted in Italy, where the emperors were also shown in the guise of a pharaoh. That is not to say that Roman Imperial interest was solely pious. Links with the religion were also a clever political means of self-promotion. Vespasian was declared Emperor whilst in Alexandria and promptly set about performing miracles there to enhance his status (cat. II).

Domitian was a keen supporter of Egyptian cults in Italy but during his reign the number of new Egyptian temple projects was disappointing. It seems likely, however, that substantial changes occurred during his reign in the presentation of two key deities: Isis and Serapis. These developments were doubtless fuelled by the gods' success in Italy. In his sanctuaries Domitian is presented with his usual portrait type on statues that for all other purposes are copied from Egyptian originals. We know that the statues were copied because of the styling of the back pillar, which is thinner than one would normally find on Egyptian statuary, even of the Roman period, and also in the way that it sits off-centre from the base and twists slightly (Ashton in McFarlane and Morgan eds. Forthcoming). It would seem then, that Roman artists were producing images of their emperor as an Egyptian pharaoh using Egyptian models. The sanctuaries of Domitian in Italy were filled with earlier sculpture (Lembke 1994 and Müller 1971) including Ptolemaic Egyptian statuary with Greek portrait features and a sphinx dating to the Twenty-sixth dynasty. Such relics were accompanied by Egyptianising columns, architectural elements and sculpture. The overall effect must have been quite splendid and it is easy to see why many Romans were attracted to Egyptian cults. There is one emperor, however, who stands apart from all others in his relationship with Egypt: Hadrian.

fig. I basalt statue of an Apis bull, Alexandria

Hadrian visited Egypt for a period of around eight to ten months in AD 130-31. This must have been an important occasion for both the province and the emperor. The capital, Alexandria, was a natural starting point for the Imperial tour, particularly given Hadrian's well-known love of Greek culture. Recent excavations and surveys of the city suggest that it was not the bastion of Greek traditions that the modern classical scholar surmises. The Ptolemaic and Roman capital had more than its fair share of Egyptian monuments and buildings, and as the Ptolemaic period progressed the city became more Egyptian in appearance than Greek (Ashton in Hirst and Silk eds. 2004). Hadrian continued the policies of the later Ptolemaic rulers by rebuilding the Serapeum (Temple of Serapis) and so associating himself with the god. The style, however, was Egyptian rather than Greek, as it had originally been. An inscription on a statue of the Apis bull (fig. I), who appears in his Egyptian form rather than an image of the Hellenised/Romanised god Sarapis/Serapis (cat. 19), shows that Hadrian dedicated a sanctuary to the Egyptian god at the site. The architectural fragments from the Serapeum are also notable, consisting of red granite columns and architraves, which replaced the earlier white marble classical columns. It is also possible that the many earlier Egyptian statues were moved to the site during this period in order to increase the Egyptian ambience there. Such material sat alongside the more traditional Roman architecture that formed the monumental main temple structure, if the coin images are to be believed. Whether or not the structure resembled the pantheon in Rome, as has been suggested, remains to be proven by a detailed survey of the site and its remains (Arnold 1999: 264 and for the plans of the site see Rowe 1942: pl. XXXII).

Hadrian made use of the riots and destruction in Alexandria immediately prior to his visit and placed a firm political message upon the province's capital with a new building programme. Hadrian's close relationship with the capital and its temples is celebrated on Alexandrian coins minted after his stay (cat. 16) and his relationship with Egypt was celebrated at his villa outside Rome (Ashton forthcoming 2006).

There is overwhelming evidence for a close connection between Hadrian and Memphis, and it was perhaps a city with which he felt both an emotional as well as ideological attachment. It must have been one of the last sites that he visited with Antinous before the ill-fated voyage and death of the youth (cat. 108-09). Birley suggests that Hadrian himself did not visit Memphis, even though there are two possible links between the emperor and the city. Firstly there was a temple dedicated to him there, and secondly Lucian associates Pachrates (an Egyptian priest who accompanied Hadrian) with the city (Weber 1907: 258). The only possible scenario that Birley suggests is that Hadrian might have visited the sanctuary of Imhotep/Asklepios on account of his fears for his health (Birley 1997: 245). Hadrian was, however, aware of the city on account of the Apis bull. Following its death in AD 128, there had been a dispute over the selection of a new bull and Hadrian had been consulted by the priests (Thompson 1988: 273). In addition to these facts, the sculptures from the emperor's villa outside Rome (Villa Adriana) may well indicate more than a passing interest in the site and will be the focus of a new study (Ashton forthcoming 2006).

In Egypt there were a small number (when compared to Augustus) of Hadrianic dedications. One can be found at the temple at Luxor in Egypt's south. In 124 AD a small chapel was built to Isis, Serapis and Zeus Helios at Luxor (fig. 2) (Arnold 1999: 264). The shrine was mud-brick and timber. Inside a white marble statue of the goddess Isis in her Romanised form (fig. 3) was dedicated and worshipped. This is a reversal of the material from Hadrian's Villa outside Rome, and an addition that is somewhat out of place in a traditional Egyptian temple complex, but not unprecedented; there is a similar statue of the god Sarapis in his Roman form at Kom Ombo. Further south, at the Temple

fig. 2 Temple of Isis, Serapis and Zeus Helios, Luxor

of Isis at Philae, Hadrian added a monumental gateway (Arnold 1999: 264 and note 81 for earlier bibliography).

Some modern writers have suggested that Egypt was simply another province to Hadrian, and that its treatment at the Villa was identical to the other regions that interested the Emperor, adding nothing more than a cosmopolitan embellishment (Macdonald and Pinto 1995: 151). There is of course always a danger of the modern scholar appropriating the sculpture from there to fit his or her own wider interpretation of the site. It is also likely that subsequent owners of the Villa may not have viewed or indeed used the material in the same way that Hadrian had originally intended. The reception of Egypt and the Egyptian material at Hadrian's Villa outside Rome has suffered because of its very nature, which is alien to the classical world. Unlike many of the scholars studying the material today Hadrian had an intimate knowledge of Egypt and, the aforementioned priest as his guide (Birley 1997: 244-45). Both the death of Antinous (cat. 108-09) and the subsequent months that the Emperor remained in order to found the city that would be dedicated to his young lover-Antinoopolis- and the cult that would celebrate his life and death, seem to have had a profound effect upon the emperor.

fig. 3 Statue of Isis

Continuing his predecessor's enthusiasm for Egypt Antoninus Pius is also notable on account of the number of dedications during his reign (Arnold 1999: 265-70). Projects mainly concentrated in Upper Egypt and Western Desert, at Kharga and Siwa. Some of the buildings were Egyptian, including a Temple to Anuket at Kommir and an Isis chapel at el-Hilla, both of which lie south and southeast of the better known Temple of Esna. An entrance kiosk was added to the Temple of Amun at Medinat Habu at Thebes and there is a gateway at Armant, part of which is still

fig. 4 Gate of Antoninus Pius,
Armant

standing (fig. 4) amongst the houses of the modern village. Both the Theban and Armant projects involved the re-use of earlier stone blocks, in the case of the latter those of the temple of Cleopatra VII. Elsewhere, however, we find buildings that were purely Roman in form. A Roman-style temple, probably to Serapis, was built at Tuna el-Gebel and the Siwan temple was of the Greek Doric order (Arnold 1999: 267-68). Both the re-using of blocks and the inclusion of non-Egyptian architecture represent a change from maintaining the buildings and images of earlier rulers for political reasons. Whereas Augustus' name and image were added to those of the Ptolemies, by the mid-second century AD it was a case of out with the old and in with the new. Such actions may well be linked to the economy and may have been the decision of the masons and priests. One of the largest projects during the reign of Antoninus Pius was executed in Alexandria, where a huge hippodrome was built, incorporating gateways of the sun and moon.

The archaeological record can often be misleading, as noted in the case of Augustus. The same is true of Caracalla's one of the few Roman emperors to adopt the Ptolemaic tradition of showing his Roman portrait on a statue that presented him as pharaoh. In AD 215, the Alexandrian's angered the emperor by suggesting that he had been involved in the murder of his brother Geta (Bowman 1990: 43-44). His response was to dismiss the Prefect, exile all Egyptians from Alexandria, making an exception for those who were engaged in running of it. The Egyptians escaped lightly: the emperor also ordered all youths in the city to be slaughtered. Such accusations and responses are documented much earlier in Alexandria, one need look no further than Cleopatra and her ancestors for a similar relationship between ruler and state. The Roman pharaohs may have been absent, in most instances never even setting foot on Egyptian soil, but in spite of this their willingness to continue as pharaoh enabled the native Egyptian culture to survive for three-hundred years after the death of the last resident ruler.

Absent Pharaohs

I. Silver denarius of Augustus (27 BC-AD 14)

Diameter 19 mm
Weight 3.89 g
28 BC
Uncertain Italian mint
CM.1487-1963

Obv. Portrait head of Octavian facing left; behind the head is a *lituus* and around the edges of the coin is the Latin legend: CAESAR-COS VI (Consul for the sixth time).

Rev. A crocodile facing right with the legend in Latin reading: above: AEGVPTO, below: CAPTA (on the conquest of Egypt).

The crocodile represents Egypt. Such coins were minted outside the province following Octavian's victory and the defeat of Mark Antony and Cleopatra VII at the battle of Actium (31 BC). Octavian became the first Roman Emperor- Augustus- in 27 BC.

RIC I, 275b

2. Copper alloy dupondius of Augustus (27 BC-AD 14)

Diameter 28.1 mm
Weight 12.99 g
9/8-3 BC
Nemausus mint
CM.69-1948

Obv. Portraits of the Emperor Augustus (right) with the general Agrippa (left) back to back. Accompanied by the Latin legend: IMP/DIVI F, above and below the heads.

Rev. A crocodile tethered to a palm tree by a chain. Below the animal are two ears of corn, perhaps representing Egypt's prosperity and above is a laurel wreath symbolising victory. Accompanied by the Latin legend: COL-NEM,

Agrippa commanded the fleet on the side of Octavian at the battle of Actium and is rewarded here by Augustus. Coins such as these and cat. I were only minted outside Egypt. These coins circulated in Gaul (Williams in Walker and Higgs eds. 260 no. 305-6).

RPC I, 524

3. Billon tetradrachm of Commodus (AD 180-192)

Diameter 26 mm
Weight 12.05 g
AD 188/189
Alexandria mint
CM.LS.2078-R

Obv. Laureate head of Commodus facing right. Accompanied by the Greek legend: M A KOM ΑΝΤΩ- CEB EVCEB.

Rev. A ship under sail with a flag at the masthead. To the left is a representation of the famous lighthouse of Alexandria, called the Pharos. The structure has a door at its base and is surmounted by lantern and a statue. The three tiers of the Pharos are shown with a square base, octagonal central section and round upper floor. A statue of Zeus is known to have been placed on the top and there are two tritons, positioned at either side of the lantern.

Egypt was essentially a source of grain for the Roman armies, which was why it became such an important province. The Alexandrian harbours were easily accessible from Mediterranean ports and so although Alexandria was no longer home to the rulers of Egypt it maintained an important administrative and trading role.

In exergue is the date [L]KΘ = year 29 of Commodus' regnal dating.

SNG pl. XLVIII.2078

4. Limestone statue of Alexander the Great

Height 59 cm
First or second century AD
Said to be from Hermopolis Magna
Purchased through the Greg Fund
GR.69.1970

The right arm is missing and the left arm is preserved to the elbow. The base is restored. The back of the base and cloak are roughly finished suggesting that the statue was positioned with its back to a wall. There is an iron dowel in the right shoulder joint (possibly ancient) and there are patches of organic staining on the cloak at the front and back, the face and the right side of the statue. Part of the right side of the hair is missing.

This statue is thought to be of a type similar to that of the original cult statue of Alexander in Alexandria. It shows the ruler and god wearing a Macedonian *chlamys*, which was the same shape as the harbour in Alexandria. The cloak is made from animal skin and is decorated around the edges with snakes; additional protection is offered in the form of the Medusa head decorating the left breast. This attribute is called an *aegis* and was associated with the gods Zeus and Athena. This form of statue is known as the Alexander Aigiochos (Stewart 1993: 246-52 no. 82-83). The portrait type is that of the deified Alexander, idealised and youthful in form. The parting of the ruler's hair to form an uplifted wave, *anastole*, is also characteristic of the type.

The manufacturing technique and style of this statue place it within the Roman rather than the Ptolemaic period as suggested in previous publications. This is not surprising since Alexander was revered during both times. Indeed when Octavian (the future emperor Augustus) visited the tomb following his conquest of Egypt in 30 BC, he is said to have bent to embrace the corpse of the hero, thereby knocking off his nose. There is no mention of Hadrian visiting the tomb in AD 130/131, and it has been suggested that either the hero was no longer deemed to be relevant enough to have been mentioned, which is very hard to believe, or, alternatively that the tomb had been destroyed during one of the riots during the first century and half of Roman rule.

Alexander the Great conquered Egypt in 332 BC. He remained there for only a matter of weeks, journeying to the Oracle of Ammon (Egyptian Amun) at Siwa in the Western Desert and then founding the city of Alexandria. After his death in Babylon in 323 BC Alexander's kingdom was divided amongst his generals, with Ptolemy, son of Lagos, taking control of Egypt. During his life Alexander had expressed a wish to be buried at Siwa but his successors decided that his body should be taken to his native Macedonia in northern Greece. Ptolemy, however, believed that his leader should be returned to Egypt and so hi-jacked the funeral cortège. Initially he laid the body to rest in Memphis, but subsequently he built a tomb in Alexandria, which would become the centre of the cult of Alexander and later of the Ptolemaic dynastic cult. Ptolemy II joined his own cult of the sibling gods to that of Alexander's but for an unknown reason kept the cult of his parents separate. During the rebuilding of the site during the reign of Ptolemy IV, the cult of Ptolemy I and his wife, Berenike I, was joined to that of Alexander and the subsequent Ptolemaic rulers. At this time a pyramid was placed over the top of the tomb, either invoking Egyptian traditions, or simply following the Hellenistic Greek fashions of the period.

Vassilika 1998: 70-71 no. 33.

Further Reading: Smith 1988: 57-64; Stewart 1993: 243-44 and 246-52.

5. Limestone head from an Egyptian-style statue with the portrait features of Ptolemy VIII

Height 9.7 cm
Second century BC
Provenance unknown
Given by G.D. Hornblower
E. 197.1939

There is damage to the front and back of the headdress and the upper section of the crown is missing. The statuette is broken across the neck. There are numerous surface abrasions.

This small limestone head is part of a statuette representing one of the late Ptolemaic rulers. The rounded face and bloated cheeks identify the image as that of Ptolemy VIII who took the cult name *Euergetes* II ('doer of good deeds') but who was also nick-named *Physcon*, Greek for 'pot-belly' or 'fatty'. 'Fatty' ruled for two periods (170-163 and 145-116 BC), being exiled for a number of years by one of his queens, his sister Cleopatra II. He was also married to her daughter and his niece, Cleopatra III. The two women became known as Cleopatra the sister and Cleopatra the wife, and images of the three can be seen dedicating together at temples and also on stelae.

The portrait is an Egyptian version of the ruler's corpulent Greek portrait-type. We know from ancient literary sources that Ptolemy VIII was extremely over-weight, to such an extent that he rarely walked, preferring to be carried around Alexandria. The portrait may, however, represent the characteristic of *Truphe*, luxury and licentiousness: this was seen to be an altogether positive trait because it indicated a person's power and wealth.

The ruler wears the Crown of Upper Egypt, which is decorated by a small *uraeus*. This symbol represented the eye of the sun god Ra and was believed to protect the wearer, always, prior to the Roman period, either a member of the royal family or god. It is similar in style but not size to a fragment of a statue representing Ptolemy VIII in Brussels. The use of a soft limestone is unusual and, along with the size, might suggest that the Fitzwilliam's statue functioned as a model or trial piece.

From the time of Ptolemy V (204-180 BC) the rulers of Egypt were sometimes shown with their typically Greek portrait features and hairstyles on statues that were in all other respects Egyptian. Thus the traditional headdresses, costumes and the back pillar that is typically found on striding statues of this period were all retained. This phenomenon resulted in statues becoming bi-lingual, in that both a Greek and an Egyptian audience could understand them. For the Egyptians the symbols of kingship were present and for the Greeks the identifying portrait of an individual was incorporated.

Further Reading: Smith 1988: 92-97; Ashton 2001: 22-23, 28-29, 90-91 and 86-87; Stanwick 2002: 57-59, 71-74 and 82; Ashton in Tait ed. 2003: 217-19.

6. Steatite Herm with the head of Ptolemy XV

Height 15 cm (without modern base 12.4 cm)
46/44-30 BC
Said to be from Koptos
Purchased through the Museums Libraries and Archives Purchase Grant Fund and the Greg Fund
E.I.2003

There are some surface abrasions and an area of substantial loss at the back and edge of the herm. The phallus and arm tenons are missing.

This form of statue with a tapering rectangular base is known as a herm, because early examples in Greece often had the head of the Greek god Hermes. They are usually decorated with a phallus, which is missing from this example but for which there is a worked socket. The holes at the sides of the statue would originally have held tenons. There are traces of copper corrosion products in the left tenon and phallus sockets, perhaps suggesting that these features were copper alloy.

This is one of a small group of statues featuring Ptolemy XV (Ashton 2001: 30-32). He can be distinguished by his youthful portrait features, forward-combed hair and the twisted royal *diadem* on his head. Although the portrait and hair on such a small scale are difficult to link to a specific ruler, both fit comfortably into the late Ptolemaic or early Roman periods (late first century BC to early first century AD). The diadem, however appears on a larger herm (now in Museo Civico, Bologna) which has been associated with the last Ptolemaic ruler, Ptolemy XV, who was the son of Cleopatra VII and Julius Caesar. He is perhaps better known by his nick-name Caesarion or 'little Caesar'.

Hard-stone statues with Greek portrait types and in an essentially Greek form, such as this, are rare in Ptolemaic Egypt. In addition to the Bologna statue, there is a fragment (a head and shoulder) in The Brooklyn Museum of Art, a head in the Petrie Museum of Egyptian Archaeology and three differently sized examples in the Egyptian Museum Cairo, two of which are manufactured in limestone and one in granite. One has a provenance indicating that this type of image was manufactured in Egypt, where it probably served a cult purpose.

At Koptos, a shrine to the god Geb was built by Cleopatra VII and an unidentified male consort (Ashton in Walker and Ashton 2003: 25-26). Scholars disagree over which ruler accompanies the queen: her father Ptolemy XII or one of her brothers (Ptolemies XIII and XIV).

Further Reading: Ashton 2001: 30-32, 68 and 98-99 no. 32.

7. Faience inlay with the portrait features of emperor Tiberius

Height 7.2 cm
First century AD (AD 14-37)
Provenance unknown
Bequeathed by C.S. Ricketts and C.H. Shannon
GR.115.1937

The nose is chipped and there are breaks around the neck. Very little of the original surface of the back survives.

This small inlay shows the usual youthful portrait type of the ruler with strong nose, prominent brow, and thin lips accentuating the downturn of the mouth, resulting in a rather supercilious appearance. This portrait type compares well with sculpture in the round (Rose 1997: 188-89; Kiss 1984: 42-45 and 138-40, no. 63-66 and 69-73).

The head is interesting because in terms of its manufacture it is similar to a frontal rather than profile portrait of Tiberius' predecessor, Augustus, now in the Metropolitan Museum of Art, New York (Wypyski in Friedman ed. 1998: 265). Both were manufactured using the self-glazing technique, which dates back to the Pre-Dynastic period in Egypt. The Fitzwilliam Museum inlay is in fact the last securely datable example of this form of faience production in Egypt. In composition it is quite different to the later Roman faience (cat. 75), which has a much paler and grittier core of crushed quartz, with an applied vitreous glaze. We know from Sir William Matthew Flinders Petrie's excavations at Kom Helul in Memphis that at least from the mid-first century AD Roman faience was massed produced by different manufacturing techniques from that used here (Ashton 2003: 44-45 and 53-58).

Tiberius was not a fan of Egyptian cults, closing down the Iseum (Temple of Isis) Campense in Rome following a scandal: it is reported that all the statues were thrown into the river Tiber. The ruler decreed that his image should not be placed with those of the gods and as such it is difficult to see how he was able fully to assimilate his Imperial role with that of the pharaoh. Several building projects were undertaken in Egypt during his reign, but it is not known whether these were simply completions of the prolific building programme of Tiberius' adoptive father, Augustus. However, work was undertaken at Philae, Medamoud and Denderah, all of which are in the southern part of Egypt (Arnold 1999: 248-50).

Vassilika 1998: 110-11 no. 53

Further reading: Rose 1997: 22-31; Bianchi in Friedman ed. 1998: 200 no. 263 (on the Metropolitan Museum's Augustus); Ashton 2003: 41.

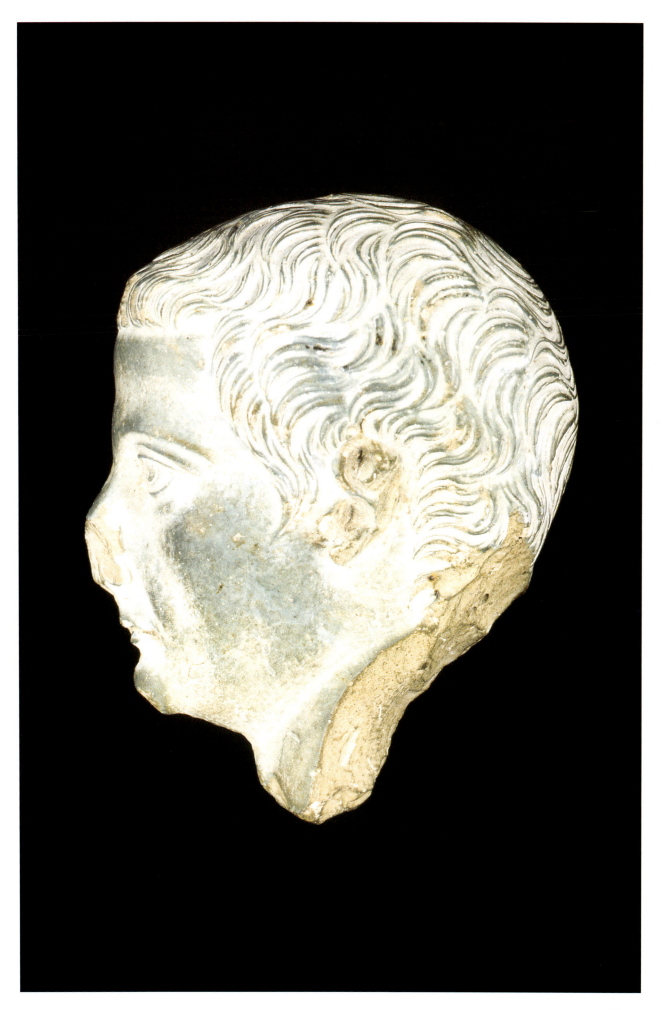

8. Limestone stela mentioning the cult of the emperor Nero

Height 25 cm
First century AD (AD54-68)
Provenance listed as Lykopolites in the Museum records
E.49.1901

The upper left section and top of the stela are missing and it is broken at the bottom. There is some surface abrasion and the text and upper register are crudely carved into the stone. There are traces of red pigment in the text. The back of the stela is roughly finished and a ledge running vertically suggests that this is a re-used architectural block.

According to Egyptian ideology, Egypt needed a king for order (*Ma'at*) to prevail. On his succession each new Roman emperor was instantly adopted to fulfil this role. Initially, the Romans were reluctant pharaohs, not keen to be worshipped as part of Egyptian cults (cat. 7). In spite of this a number of building projects continued from the start of the Roman period and the new rulers were often shown as pharaohs. This relationship was mutually beneficial to both ruler and priests because the latter needed a king to rule and the king needed the support and promotion that he received from the temples. The relationship between the two was not always quite so simple and some of the new Roman rulers were seen to take away wealth and power of the prominent Egyptian priesthoods.

This stela is interesting in presenting an Egyptian scene in the top register, accompanied by a Greek inscription. Greek continued to be the main language of administration in Egypt following Roman occupation. The inscription reads: *For the Tyche of Nero Claudius Caesar Augustus Germanicus Imperator, the Synod* [*of the...*]. Tyche, the goddess of Fortune, and by association the use of Tyche or agathos (good) Tyche on inscriptions such as this implies the (good) fortune of the subject. As early as the Ptolemaic period it was common for such dedications to invoke Tyche for the benefit of the king and its use here on a stela to the emperor Nero is a continuation of this tradition.

The scene at the top of the stela is roughly carved in relief and shows two jackals, probably representing the god Anubis, separated by an ankh, the symbol of life. Pairs were often favoured by the Romans and the two jackals may well be a reference to this artistic preference. On the other hand in earlier Theban tombs two jackals are often depicted, perhaps representing the gods Anubis and Wepwawet (Strudwick and Strudwick 1996: 51-56). The winged sun-disk which decorated the rounded top is a traditional Egyptian feature, serving a protective function. This symbolism suggests that the stela may have served a funerary rather than a simply votive purpose.

Towards the end of Nero's reign a rebellion took place in Alexandria. The catalyst had been disagreements between the Greek and Jewish communities there. The Roman army was sent into Egypt to quash the rebellion and it is recorded that 50,000 Alexandrians were killed. Elsewhere in Egypt, however, temples continued to be built, still featuring the emperor Nero as king.

Martin forthcoming

9. Billon tetradrachm of Nero (AD 54-68)

Diameter 25 mm
Weight 12.93 g
AD 65
Alexandria mint
CM.LS.2046-R

Obv. Portrait bust of Nero who faces to the viewer's right. The emperor wears the aegis of Zeus and the radiate crown associated with the sun god Helios. The portrait is accompanied by the Greek legend: ΝΕΡΩ ΚΛΑΥ ΚΑΙΣ ΣΕΒ ΓΕΡ,

Rev. Bust of Alexandria. The personification can be identified by the elephant headdress and chlamys (Macedonian cloak). The harbour and coastline of Alexandria was similar in shape to this cloak, which often appeared on representations of Alexander the Great, founder of the city (cat. 4). The bust is accompanied by the Greek legend: ΑΥΤΟ-ΚΡΑ.

In the right field is the date L IB = year 12 of Nero's regnal dating.

SNG: pl. XLVI.2046

10. Billon tetradrachm of Vespasian (AD 69-79)

Diameter 24 mm
Weight 12.63 g
AD 69
Alexandria mint
CM.G.2-R

Obv. Laureate head of the emperor Vespasian facing right. Accompanied by the Greek legend: ΑΥΤ ΤΙΤ ΦΛΑΥΙ ΟΥΕΣΠΑΣΙΑΝ ΚΑΙΣ and the date LA= year 1 of Vespasian's regnal dating.

Rev. A personification of the city of Alexandria standing facing left. The goddess wears an elephant headdress; in her out-stretched right hand she holds a laurel wreath and in her left a sceptre.

The wreath corresponds with that worn by the emperor on the obverse of the coin and implies that he is crowned by Alexandria. The scene is accompanied by the Greek legend: ΑΛΕΞΑΝ-[ΔΡΕΙΑ]. Vespasian was declared Emperor whilst in Egypt and so it is likely that such coins had a special relevance to this particular ruler.

Milne 386

II. Meta-Basalt head from a statue of the emperor Vespasian

Height 10.5 cm
First century AD (AD 79-69)
Provenance unknown. Given to Sir Robert Greg by Howard Carter, thus likely to be from Egypt
Bequeathed by Sir Robert Greg
E.83.1954

There is damage to the forehead, nose, mouth and chin. There is a further eroded section at the back of the head covering the left ear. The top of the head was finished with the present flat surface and inserted into a headdress made in another material or stone. The inlays for the eyes are missing and the statue is broken at the neck.

Not all scholars agree that this head represents the emperor Vespasian; some prefer to identify it as a portrait of a private individual. However, the closely set eyes, loose fleshy lips and lines around the cheeks and eyes are all features of the emperor's Roman portrait type. During the first and second centuries AD Roman emperors often appear as pharaohs but without the usual regalia. The *uraeus* (protective cobra) is often missing from the brow, or the rulers appear without the typical headdress. This movement began during the reign of the last Ptolemaic ruler (see cat. 6). Earlier Ptolemaic portraits are always accompanied by the correct attributes so that they could be understood by an Egyptian audience (cat. 5).

This type of portrait is also found in Egypt, perhaps most notably in the Middle Kingdom representations of the kings Senusret III and Amenemhat III. As a type, it is often termed 'veristic' or 'realistic' because it is non-idealised, showing signs of age. However, it is highly unlikely that such images in Egypt can be regarded as lifelike representations of the subject. It is generally thought that such images rather portray a message of maturity or wisdom. Interestingly officials are often allocated the same features as the current ruler, the only difference being that a private individual is not given divine or royal attributes.

Vespasian was declared emperor in Egypt in AD 69 whilst serving there with the army. His father was a tax collector and money lender, his mother the sister of a senator. As such he was ill-equipped to fulfil the divine role of pharaoh. Soon after his elevation to power, however, Vespasian saw a vision during a visit to Alexandria and is reported to have performed a miracle in his capacity as Serapis at the site (Suetonius *Vespasian* 7). Divinity in hand, Vespasian returned to Rome, but his policy of increasing taxation was not popular in the provinces. Two other portraits of the ruler in an Egyptian style but showing the same portrait features as the Fitzwilliam Museum's statue fragment both take the form of a sphinx. One is in the Ny Carlsberg Glyptotek and the other is in the Egyptian Museum Cairo (Kiss 1984: fig. 96-97). In spite of Vespasian's connections with Egypt there is little evidence of temple building during his rule, though fragments from an unknown temple of the period were found re-used in a Roman fort (Arnold 1999: 260). The ruler had two sons, who expressed an interest in Egyptian culture. Titus attended the ceremony to inaugurate the new Apis Bull at Memphis (cat. 99) on his father's behalf and Domitian was a well-known Egyptophile (cat. 12).

Vassilika 1995: 132-33 no. 62

Further Reading: Kiss 1984: 50-52 and 145-47 no. 88-99.

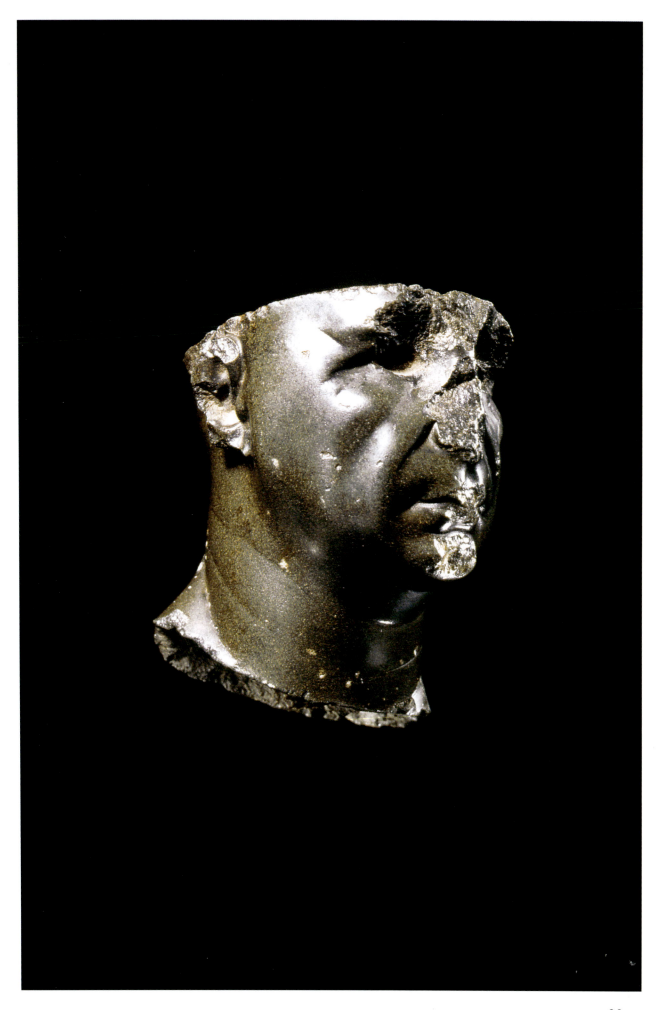

12. Sandstone relief showing the Emperor Domitian as pharaoh

Height 14.8 cm, Width 25.5 cm
First century AD (AD 81-96)
Provenance unknown, perhaps Aswan
Purchased through the Greg Fund
E.1.2003

The upper left and right edges are missing from the block and there is a substantial loss to the surface above the head of the ram. There are traces of plaster preserved in the carved hieroglyphs and two different shades of yellow pigment.

This fragment of a temple relief shows Domitian on the viewer's right making an offering to the ram-headed god Khnum. The emperor carries a sceptre in the form of a god (possibly Heh, the god of eternity). The hieroglypic inscription reads '...of Amun-Ra' and is accompanied by a cartouche spelling 'Caesar' and then the emperor's name.

Domitian is well known for his patronage of Egyptian cults in Italy, but only four known temple projects were undertaken in Egypt during his reign. This relief probably came from one in Aswan that was dedicated to the triad Khnum, Satet and Anuket. It was destroyed during the early nineteenth century. Although the text mentions Amun-Ra, there are no known temples to this god dedicated by the emperor. We must therefore assume that the prominent position of Khnum in the relief offers a clue to the original dedication. The other temples known to have been associated with this particular emperor were built at Hermopolis Magna in Middle Egypt (to the goddess Nehemet-awy), at el-Dush in the Kharga Oasis (dedicated to Isis, Serapis and Horus). In addition to these two small-scale projects a gateway was added to the north wall of the temple of Hathor at Denderah. The only other possible provenance of the Fitzwilliam Museum's fragment is a Temple to an unknown deity at Kom el-Resras, which is located on the west bank of the river Nile, approximately 30 km north of Kom Ombo (Arnold 1999: 262, note 69). This site was not fully excavated, but blocks belonging to a temple of Domitian were noted (Sayce 1907: 102-5).

The Emperor Domitian's interest in Egypt is perhaps best expressed through his Italian sanctuaries dedicated to the goddess Isis in Rome (Lembke 1994) and Benevento (Müller 1971). At both sites the emperor is shown in Egyptian guise with his usual Roman portrait type, continuing a tradition that was started by the Ptolemies (cat. 5 and cat. 6). Statues were imported and made specially to decorate the sanctuaries and it is thought that during this particular emperor's reign the iconography of the goddess Isis was developed and modified from its original Egyptian form.

Further reading: Müller 1971; Kiss 1984: no. 52-53 no. 100-01; Lembke 1994; Arnold 1999: 260-63.

13. Billon tetradrachm of Trajan (AD 98-117)

Diameter 24.2 mm
Weight 12.33 g
AD 115/6
Alexandria mint
CM.G.5-R

Obv. A bust of Trajan facing right. The Emperor wears a crown of sun-rays linking him to the sun god Helios. Accompanied by the Greek legend: [...]ΑΡΙ CE-B ΓΕΡΜ ΔΑ[...].

Rev. A bust of the god Serapis facing right. The god can be identified by his long wavy hair and beard and distinguished from Nilus by the *modius* or grain measure on top of his head. Serapis was a popular god and was often closely associated with the Roman emperors just as he had been linked to the early Ptolemaic rulers.

In the field is the date LI- Θ = year 19 of Trajan's regnal dating.

Compare Milne 629

14. Copper alloy drachm of Hadrian (AD 117-138)

Diameter 34 mm
Weight 22.66 g
AD 120/121
Alexandria mint
CM.675-1948

Obv. Laureate portrait of Hadrian facing right, with drapery on left shoulder. Accompanied by the Greek legend: AVT KAI TPAI-AΔPIA CEB.

Rev. Hadrian stands in an elephant-drawn quadriga facing right. The emperor holds a sceptre in his left hand and palm branch in his right.

Before the scene is the date LE = year 5 of Hadrian's regnal dating.

Milne 997

33

15. Silver drachm of Hadrian (AD 117-138)

Diameter 35 mm
Weight 30.14 g
AD 130/131
Alexandria mint
CM.LS.2062-R

Obv. Laureate, draped and cuirassed bust of Hadrian, shown as if viewed from the back. Accompanied by the Greek legend: AVT KAI–TPAI AΔPIA CEB.

Rev. Hadrian stands facing left. He wears a toga and holds a sceptre in his left hand, his right hand is raised towards a personification of Alexandria, who faces the Emperor. The goddess wears a short *chiton* (dress) and an elephant headdress; in her left hand are two ears of corn.

Hadrian visited Egypt in AD 130/131 and remained in the country for several months. During this time we know that he rebuilt the city of Alexandria following riots there. This coin may well be a reference to the Emperor's extended stay in the city.

Low in the field is the date L-IE = year 15 of Hadrian's regnal dating.

SNG: pl. XLVII.2062

16. Copper alloy drachm of Hadrian (AD 117-138)

Diameter 32 mm
Weight 23.52 g
AD 132/133
Alexandria mint
CM.G.7-R

Obv. A laureate bust of Hadrian with drapery on left shoulder. Accompanied by the Greek legend: AYT KAIC TPAIAN-AΔPI[ANOC C]EB.

Rev. Serapis and Hadrian stand in a di-style temple, consisting of two Corinthian columns and a pediment with a central disk motif. To the left stands Serapis, wearing a *modius* (grain measure) and holding a long sceptre. The god raises his right hand in an act of blessing the figure to the right- Hadrian. The emperor holds a long sceptre with his left hand and places his right hand above an altar inscribed AΔP/IA/NON (Hadrian).

The exergue is illegible but probably year 17 of Hadrian's regnal dating. This scene is particularly relevant to this Emperor following his visit to Egypt in AD 130/131.

Milne 1379

17. Billon tetradrachm of Antoninus Pius (AD 138-161)

Diameter 27 mm
Weight 13.71 g
AD 159/160
Alexandria Mint
CM.LS.2074-R

Obv. Laureate and draped bust of Antoninus Pius facing right and seen as if viewed from the back. Accompanied by the Greek legend: ANTΩNINO-CEB EVCE·.

Rev. Facing busts of Serapis, crowned with a *modius* (grain measure) and Isis, crowned with the sun-disk, cow's horns and double plumed crown, originally worn by Ptolemaic queens but adopted for the goddess during the Roman period.

Low in the field is the date LKΓ = year 23 of Antoninus Pius' regnal dating.

SNG: XLVII.2074

18. Lead medallion showing the portrait of the Emperor Marcus Aurelius

Diameter 3.2 cm
AD161-180
Oxyrhynchus
Given by the Egypt Exploration Fund
E.12.1904

The medallion has split across the centre and there is further damage to the lower edge. There are lead corrosion products on the surface and only patchy remains of an inscription at the top of the medallion. The object was stamped in the same way that a coin was manufactured, as indicated by the outer circle at the top. Two holes were then punched through from the back in order to attach it to an object. Remains of fibres are preserved in the left-side hole.

The image shows two figures facing each other. On the viewer's right is a portrait of Marcus Aurelius, with his characteristic long beard and tightly curled hair. Emperors during this period nurtured the so-called philosopher appearance, hence the beard. The thick curly hair and beard lent themselves well to representations of the Roman rulers as the god Serapis and indeed on a marble bust of this particular ruler, now in the Fitzwilliam Museum and said to be from Alexandria, the beard is parted in a manner that is closely associated with the Roman version of this god (fig. 5, see page 6).

On the left is a bust of a youthful clean-shaven male, wearing a diadem or crown on his head and a cuirass. He is probably a god. It is unlikely that he represents the co-ruler of Marcus Aurelius, Lucius Verus, because he is typically also typically shown with a beard.

Further Reading: Kiss 1984: 63-67 and 161-66 no. 139-59.

19. Limestone statue of the god Serapis

Height 56.5 cm
Second century AD?
Provenance unknown
Lent by Corpus Christi College, Lewis Collection
Temporary loan ant. 103.93

The back and section of stone supporting the dog are roughly finished. There is damage to the front of the *modius* and the left hand side of the throne; the left index finger is missing.

This seated form of the god Serapis is known as the Alexandrian type and it is often suggested that the original cult statue of the Greek Sarapis took this form (Ashton 2003: 11-13). The only surviving part of the original cult statue is the head, which is now housed in the Greco-Roman Museum in Alexandria. Literary sources describe the body as consisting of jewels and precious metals but there is no suggestion that the god was seated.

The Romans seem to have developed a slightly different version of the god. The long hair and beard were both features of the original Ptolemaic Greek version but many of the attributes such as the long garment are Roman additions. Furthermore the addition of the three headed dog Cerberus, who guarded the gateway to the underworld, and the grain measure on the god's head do not appear until the Roman period. The locks of hair on the forehead and the divided beard are also features of Roman Serapis rather than the original Sarapis.

Serapis was modelled on the Greek Sarapis, himself a Hellenised version of an existing Egyptian hybrid god. The Egyptian god consists of Osiris and Apis. Osiris was the god of the Egyptian afterlife and so the Roman underworld. Apis, a bull who actually lived at Memphis, in death was worshipped as Osiris Apis. The earliest reference to a Greek version of this cult occurs in the fourth century BC when a woman invokes the help of the god Osarapis in a Greek text (Fraser 1972: 250-51 n. 474).

The early Ptolemaic rulers built a sanctuary to Sarapis in Alexandria and there was an established centre for the god in his Egyptian form at Memphis. The Alexandrian cult was closely associated with the Ptolemaic royal family in the third century BC but following the moving of the royal court to Memphis during the reign of Ptolemy V (204-181 BC) and an apparently greater need for the rulers to be seen as Egyptian, this Hellenised god fell out of favour. Like Isis, Serapis became enormously popular in the Roman world, when once again he became linked with the Roman Emperors (Cat. 11 and 18).

Further reading: Ashton 2003: 10-13; Ashton in Hirst and Silk 2004: 22-25.

Coinage and Roman Egypt

One of the most important of the achievements of the Emperor Augustus (who was called Octavian until 27 BC) was the conquest of Egypt, the last of the Greek Hellenistic kingdoms, which had been systematically swallowed up by the Romans. The conquest was actually achieved not in Egypt itself, but at the Battle of Actium in Greece, where, under the generalship of Agrippa, Octavian's fleet defeated that of Mark Antony and Cleopatra VII. The subsequent invasion of Egypt was a small matter, when Mark Antony committed suicide. So did Cleopatra, to Octavian's disappointment, and the kingdom fell into his hands.

This accomplishment was publicised everywhere, including on coinage. A famous silver denarius of Augustus depicts the crocodile, symbol of Egypt, with the legend AEGYPTO CAPTA- on the conquest of Egypt (cat. 1). A large number of copper alloy coins struck at Nemausus in Gaul, at the other end of the Roman Empire, show the defeated crocodile shackled to a palm tree (cat. 2).

Egypt now was not added formally to the Empire, but was retained by Augustus, and his successors, as the private property of the Emperor. As a most important source of grain for Rome, Egypt had to be kept under close control, and of course the profits were considerable. To secure financial control, while emphasising the distinction in status between Egypt and the other Roman provinces, a closed economy was created by continuing the particular money system of the Ptolemaic kingdom. Under Cleopatra VII, the last of the Ptolemaic rulers, there was no gold coinage; the silver coinage was of low quality, although there was substantial copper alloy ('bronze'). This was a kind of coinage not likely to be easily accepted elsewhere.

Under Augustus the Ptolemaic coinage went on circulating within Egypt. The emperor struck copper alloy coinage on which he simply substituted his head for Cleopatra's, confirming his personal rule: for the Egyptians he was seen as the next king in succession, rather than as a foreign conqueror, a role confirmed by the number of temples dedicated and promoting his image.

Augustus' successor, Tiberius, continued the issue of base silver tetradrachms on the same system; and with Nero and subsequent emperors large quantities of these were struck, bearing the head of the emperor on the obverse and many different types on the reverse.

The wealth of Roman Egypt is not obvious from its deliberately low-grade coinage, although wealth might be suggested by the enormous quantities of coins produced. Rather, it is the repertoire of innumerable different coin types, on coinage that was to last for fully three hundred years, that gives the Romano-Egyptian coinage its particular interest.

The types are largely religious in subject, ranging indiscriminately over the whole series of gods, both Egyptian and classical, a well as depictions of their temples and their rites. The centuries-old presence of Greeks in the Late and Ptolemaic periods caused their myths too to infuse the culture, so that for example a group of large copper alloy coins struck under Antoninus Pius show the series of the Adventures of Hercules.

One curiosity of the reverse types, whether of gods or architectural structures, is that they are almost never identified by a legend (contrary to the usage on the coins of Rome itself). The implication is that the iconography was thought to be sufficiently well-known to the public, as not to need a label. However, the reverses usually carry a number, the regnal year of the emperor figured on the obverse: in this small way the emperor was himself associated with the reverse type, for example in his worship of and association with the divinity portrayed.

20. Copper alloy drachm of Trajan (AD 98-117)

Diameter 34 mm
Weight 24.18 g
AD 109/110
Alexandria mint
CM.602-1950

Obv. Laureate portrait of Trajan facing right, accompanied by the Greek legend: [AVT TP]AIAN CE-B- ΓEPM ΔAKIK.

Rev. Zeus, accompanied by an eagle to the left, stands in a di-style Corinthian temple. In the god's right hand is a thunderbolt and in the left a long sceptre. On the pediment of the temple is a disk supported by two flying figures. It is highly likely that this represented an Alexandrian temple dedicated to the god Zeus.

In the field, left and right, is the date LI-Γ = year 13 of Trajan's regnal dating

Compare Geissen 540

21. Copper alloy drachm of Trajan (AD 98-117)

Diameter 35 mm
Weight 26.62 g
AD 110/111
Alexandria mint
CM.54-1934

Obv. Laureate portrait of Trajan. By the neck is an *aegis* (a motif associated with the Greek god Zeus). Around the coin is the Greek legend: [AVT TPAIA]N C-[EB ΓEPM ΔAKIK].

Rev. Triumphal arch with three gateways; on the top is a statue of a victorious Emperor, holding laurel branch and sceptre, standing in a chariot drawn by six horses. At the sides are two trophies. It is possible that this arch represents one in Rome, or a gateway of the city of Alexandria.
In the field is the date [L]I-Δ = year 14 of Trajan's regnal dating.

Geissen 564

43

22. Copper alloy drachm of Hadrian (AD 117-138)

Diameter 32 mm
Weight 23.17 g
AD 134/135
Alexandria mint
CM.81-1924

Obv. Laureate, draped and cuirassed bust of Hadrian shown as if viewed from the back. Accompanied by the Greek legend: AVT KAIC TPAIAN-AΔPIAN[OC CEB].

Rev. Egyptian temple with two obelisks represented on either side of the door. Above the entrance is a garland and a statue of Isis, with sceptre in hand. It seems likely that this building represents an actual temple. Perhaps the closest parallels are the Temple of Horus at Edfu or the Temple of Isis at Philae (where an archway is dedicated to Hadrian). It is also possible that the temple represents one in Alexandria. Two obelisks were for example placed in front of the Temple to the Deified Julius Caesar, which was inaugurated by Cleopatra VII. Similar temples appear on the Palaestrina mosaic (Meyboom 1995: 53-60), although it is often assumed that here the temple represents a generic sanctuary rather than a specific site.

Around the temple is the date L-E-N-NE/AKΔ = year 19 of Hadrian's regnal dating.

BMC 879

23. Copper alloy drachm of Antoninus Pius (AD 138-161)

Diameter 35 mm
Weight 27.48 g
AD 144/145
Alexandria mint
CM.87-1934

Obv. Laureate head of Antoninus Pius facing right. Accompanied by the Greek legend: AVT K T AIΛ AΔP-ANTΩNINOC C-EB EVC.

Rev. Di-style Egyptian temple with papyrus columns and lotus flower capitals. The pediment is rounded and contains a sundisk and double *uraeus*. Between the columns, Isis Lactans is seated on a throne facing right, she wears a small crown and is dressed in a *chiton* and *himation*. On her knee sits her son Harpocrates, naked except for the Crowns of Upper and Lower Egypt. In his left hand he holds a lotus flower.

In field the is the date LH = year 8 of Antoninus Pius' regnal dating..

Milne 1839

24. Copper alloy drachm of Antoninus Pius (AD 138-161)

Diameter 33 mm
Weight 20.45 g
AD 151/152
Alexandria mint
CM.668-1948

Obv. Laureate head of Antoninus Pius facing left, with drapery on the right shoulder. Accompanied by the Greek legend: AVT K T AIΛ A-ΔPI-ANTΩNINOC C-EB EVC.

Rev. Tetrastyle building with antefixes at each of the front corners, and a pyre represented on top of the upper floor. This building has been identified as the Altar of the Caesareum (Temple to the Deified Julius Caesar). Between the central columns a female figure dropping incense over an altar.

In exergue is L and in the field is I-E = year 15 Antoninus Pius' regnal dating.

Compare Milne 2163

25. Copper alloy drachm of Lucius Verus (AD 161-180)

Diameter 31 mm
Weight 22.47 g
AD 168/169
Alexandria mint
CM.658-1948

Obv. Laureate head of Lucius Verus facing right. Accompanied by the Greek legend: (?) [ΛO]YKIOC-[…].

Rev. Di-style temple with what appear to be Ionic columns and pediment, at the centre of which is a sun-disk and double *uraeus*. Inside, Serapis is seated on throne facing left. On the back of the throne is the goddess Victory, Greek Nike. The god holds a sceptre in his left hand and extends his right hand to Cerberos, seated at his feet.

The temple here is a hybrid form of others found on coins. Egyptian-style buildings often have a rounded pediment decorated with the disk and cobras; however, here the pediment is of the usual triangular form. It is possible that the columns are intended to be Egyptian rather than eastern Greek but the surface of the coin is too worn to be certain.

Around the edges of the coin is the date [L E]NA-TO[V] = year 9 of Lucius Verus' regnal dating.

Geissen 2066

47

Adopting, adapting or continuing the Egyptian tradition?

It is fair to say that Egypt did not change overnight following the death of Cleopatra VII. This would have been an impossible feat, given the size of the country and the diversity of its communities who lived there. What we find as the first century BC becomes 'common era' (AD) is that some, but by no means all, material culture changed gradually. These changes started during the reign of Tiberius, the second Roman emperor, who was a somewhat reluctant pharaoh. It is not always easy to date objects accurately to the reign of a single emperor but coins and also vessels that can be dated by archaeological excavations go some way to help us understand when key changes occur. Before considering the evidence in greater detail it is necessary to acknowledge the different categories of styles with varying degrees of interaction between Egyptian and Roman that form the wider class of Romano-Egyptian culture.

Firstly we have material from Italy as well as Egypt. We also find two types of objects: firstly those that are Romano-Egyptian, that is to say Egyptian from the Roman period; and secondly a category largely, but not exclusively, from Italy, that form an Egyptianising category. Such objects are inspired by Egyptian models but are manufactured according to classical (that is to say Greek and Roman) artistic cannons. Statues are thus without a back pillar and are not constrained to a striding stance, but stand in a more natural position more typical of contemporary Roman sculpture. We also find objects such as cat. 103, which is modelled on a figure of Bes but which has become an architectural element with features that are copied from, but which do not strictly adhere to, an Egyptian model.

Within the Romano-Egyptian category we find a number of sub-categories. We have objects that continue an established tradition such as the fertility figures (cat. 90). These figures owe a considerable amount to Roman methods of manufacture and style but are essentially a continuation of a long-standing Egyptian practice. We also find objects that adapt an established Egyptian belief such as those associated with the inundation of the Nile. Traditional New Year flasks disappear and more general artifacts appear such as frog lamps (cat. 72-74) or plates with schematic representations of items associated with the annual flood (cat. 75). Such changes are often considered to represent a general degeneration of art and culture during this period, and yet what they really show is that the Egyptian tradition is still very much alive and flourishing, and more importantly still developing.

Romano-Egyptian culture also contains objects that belong to the earlier native tradition in terms of their style and manufacture, but which were re-used and, in some cases, changed their identity or meaning. In terms of their categorisation they remain true to Egypt but their changed function is more closely described as Egyptianising. This term implies a lack of understanding by either the artist responsible for the piece or on behalf of the viewer. In both instances the artist or viewer is Roman. Ancient Egyptians needed a series of attributes that they could quite literally 'read' in order to understand an object or subject. If the necessary features are present it should not really matter whether a statue is with or without a back pillar and usual stance, and this is perhaps why we find the production of classicised objects in Egypt and perhaps their use by Egyptian communities. Objects that do not adhere to the strict cannons of Egyptian artistic practices can therefore be seen as Roman versions of Egyptian artifacts. It is therefore necessary to further divide Romano-Egyptian and Egyptianising into artistic style and usage. A changed style could be used and understood in Egypt providing that the necessary attributes were present. Where perhaps some confusion did occur is when objects that once represented something quite specific according to Egyptian culture were adopted and then adapted by Romans in Italy only to be exported back their country of origin. There is one notable instance of this very phenomenon: the cult of Isis and the associated statues of the goddess. Many such images are Egyptian in form but are re-used in a novel way. We thus have Romano-Egyptian objects that can be used in an Egyptianising (i.e. none pure) way, and Egyptianising objects (i.e. those made according to classical cannons but copying Egyptian material) that can be used in a traditional manner.

The Romans imported statues of Ptolemaic queens to Rome and re-used them in sanctuaries of the goddess Isis. Statues such as cat. 29 were originally made to represent Ptolemaic queens in their deified form. However, in the first century AD they appear as images of Isis on Roman lamps and in sanctuaries in Italy (Ashton 2003: 34). The knotted garment was not exclusively used to represent Isis in Egypt, as seen from funerary contexts and also late Ptolemaic terracotta figurines perhaps representing priestesses (Walters in Bricault ed. 2000: 63). Ashton (2000, 2001 and 2003b) has agued that the knotted costume and corkscrew locks were used to represent deified Ptolemaic queens but that during the first century AD such images were taken to Rome and used as images of Isis. Statues were then re-imported into Egypt and used as representations of the goddess at sanctuaries such as the temple in Luxor (see fig. 3). In Egypt the traditional form of the goddess continued to be used on temple reliefs well into the third century AD, and it is possible that the new form of the goddess invoked an association with the original subjects of these statues, namely the cults of the Ptolemaic queens, which continued to flourish well into the Roman period.

Many other objects were imported from Italy to Egypt and copied. Lamps are one of the primary sources of imported material, with artists copying Italian forms in the local Egyptian clays and sometimes altering the decoration on the discus. Along side such enterprises we find new forms of lamp such as the aforementioned frog lamps that are Egyptian in origin.

Lamps are of considerable help in dating developments such as the iconography of Isis and Serapis, because they can be dated within a short period of time and often a single reign. Such developments are indicative of trade links between the two countries and also of the stronger cultural links that the Egypt and Italy enjoyed following the Roman conquest. The export of objects from Egypt to Italy will be further explored later in this catalogue. However, there is one further subject that should be addressed under the present heading: the myth of Greco-Roman Egypt, which was questioned by Ashton (2003: 29-37).

fig. 6 Geb shrine, Koptos

It is aspects such as the cult of Isis and her deviating iconography that prevent the validity of the term Greco-Roman when applied to objects. If the term were used simply as an abbreviation for Ptolemaic and Roman Egypt it would perhaps be more credible. Greco-Roman is, however, more widely used in describing the date of individual objects or worse still to describe the culture of later Egypt. Many handbooks on Egyptian art and history contain a short and combined chapter on the Greco-Roman period but rarely are two different earlier stages of Egyptian history lumped together in this way. Quite the opposite is true. Historians and archaeologists who specialise in earlier periods divide them into 'kingdoms' with the further division of 'intermediate periods'. Why then should Ptolemaic and Roman be combined in this way. The problem lies in the classical and so non-Egyptian aspects of their character. Just as few classicists can tell the difference between an Old Kingdom and Middle Kingdom statue, so those trained only in Egyptology naturally struggle with a discipline that essentially does not concern them. Romano-Egyptian culture in particular, which differs from Ptolemaic in that it provides the first instance of a mixing of traditions, is alien to those who study Egypt and Rome. The result of this problem is that many Romano-Egyptian objects are dismissed as modern forgeries and those that fall into an Egyptianising category are dated to the wave of Egyptomania that occurred in the eighteenth or nineteenth centuries. As we shall see, many of the objects in this catalogue could offer the first instance of this phenomenon; others are, however, the result of new developments in Egyptian culture- a literal breaking of the old mould.

In Egypt, the most obvious immediate changes of the Roman regime were seen on new building projects of traditional Egyptian temples. Here, Augustus replaced Cleopatra as the new pharaoh. It cannot, however, be merely a coincidence that wherever the Queen dedicated so did her successor; whilst there was a certain amount of finishing off earlier building projects there are some notable new buildings close to where Cleopatra dedicated. At Koptos the Geb shrine that contained relief decorations of Cleopatra VII on the inside was 'finished' with representations of Augustus (fig. 6). At Denderah, where the south wall of the Temple of Hathor contains one of Cleopatra's best known images, a small shrine to Hathor-Isis was decorated with the image of the new pharaoh (fig. 7). This observation brings us to another division within the culture of Roman Egypt: official versus private. Within this field we must also ask the question of the extent to which a foreign non-resident and in many cases non-visiting pharaoh could have on the production of Egyptian material culture in the Roman period. We have already seen with regard to the goddess Isis that it was possible for new forms of gods to be accepted into Egyptian temples and homes, but the degree of influence in many other instances was not always a direct result of Roman interference. Changes in the financing of temples and cults had a clear effect on the types of objects that were dedicated and so manufactured. The fluctuation of the more general economy may also indirectly have forced certain changes in Egypt during the first and second centuries AD.

fig. 7 birth house of Hathor-Isis at Denderah (left)

Firstly, and most notably, faience started to be mass produced with less care taken over the manufacture of individual objects. This material had always had a close association with the king and related royal cults. The change occurred during the reign of Tiberius thus allowing one generation of a continued tradition before the changes kicked in. The kinds of objects that were produced were also transformed during this period. We find predominantly bowls that copy imported forms of Italian pottery being produced at sites such as Memphis. Some figures of gods continued to be produced but these seem simply to be alternatives for terracotta figures; in form they are the same the only difference being that a vitreous glaze rather than plaster and paint was applied. The last known faience object associated with the old manufacturing techniques and subject (in the form of the Roman portrait of the ruler) is a head of Tiberius (cat. 7). This change is supported by the dating of the new form of the material (Ashton 2003: 39-58).

We also find a notable decrease in the production of Egyptian-style royal images. These tend to follow either a generic form showing the pharaoh or, on occasion represent the ruler with his portrait features according to the Roman style but wearing the attributes of a pharaoh. Oddly, many of these images from Egypt show the ruler without the protective *uraeus* or cobra. There are also no real references to Imperial women within the Egyptian tradition which is a notable change when their predecessor the Ptolemaic queens are considered. Temples, however, continued to be dedicated but even here we often find the name of the Roman pharaoh is commonly replaced with the more general cartouche spelling the Egyptian word in hieroglyphs (fig. 8). The Egyptian priesthood and Egypt needed a king in order to preserve the unity and calm of the country and in a similar way the Roman emperors, even the reluctant pharaohs, clearly understood the power of promoting their image to the higher levels of Egyptian society. Some, such as Hadrian, took a genuine interest in Egypt and Egyptian cults, employing an Egyptian priest during his stay to advise him. Ultimately, the absence of the emperors did not really seem to present a problem for the continuity of the Egyptian tradition, but it did have a profound effect upon Egyptian culture.

fig. 8 temple relief, Armant

Isis

26. Faience statuette of Isis nursing Horus

Height 13. 5 cm
Late Period
Bequeathed by C.S. Rickets and C. H. Shannon
E.60.1937

There is some surface loss at the front of the base and further patches of surface damage to the wig and arms. It is possible that some of the surface loss is a result of the firing and glazing process. The larger figure is broken through the centre of the body and has been repaired. The feet of the smaller figure are missing.

This mould-made faience figurine shows the seated goddess Isis nursing her son Horus (Harpocrates). The goddess appears in the usual sheath-like Egyptian dress and is identified by the throne hieroglyph on her head, which literally spells her name. Her wig is the traditional Egyptian tri-partite form worn by many goddesses and queens. In addition to wearing the throne as a crown, Isis is also commonly shown with the sun disk and cow's horns (cat. 32).

Isis was the mother of Horus (personified by the living king) and the consort of the god Osiris (associated with the deceased king): as such she was linked to fertility and is also often shown in a protective form, often with wings. Here we see her in her role as mother. The young Horus is shown as a small adult, wearing a cap and with a side lock indicating his youth. The finger to mouth pose was also one that was associated with children and this particular feature also appears on representations of Harpocrates in the form of a chubby child on terracotta figurines from the Roman period. There is a panel filled with a lotus design on each side of the throne on which the goddess sits.

Further reading: Krauss 1980: 186-203; Westendorf 1980: 204.

27. Copper Alloy coin of Cleopatra VII (51-30 BC)

Diameter 27 mm
Weight 15.76 g
47-38 BC (?)
Cyprus mint
CM.MC.9846-R

Obv. Bust of Cleopatra VII wearing the divine *stephane* (crown) and holding a sceptre, visible behind her head. In front of the queen is a small infant, thought to be her son by the Roman Julius Caesar. Here, the pair is assimilated to Isis and Horus but appear in a wholly Greek manner.

Rev. A double cornucopia, joined at bottom and bound with fillet; in the field, to the right is the monogram: ΚΛΕΟΠΑΤΡΑΣ-ΒΑΣΙΛΙΣΣΗΣ.

Cleopatra VII and Arsinoe II are the only two Ptolemaic queens to use the double form of cornucopia. Its appearance on coins has helped scholars to identify statues of the two queens. It is possible that these coins were minted to celebrate the birth of Ptolemy XV. They are the only coins to show the queen with one of her children; she usually appears alone (in Egypt) or with Mark Antony on some of the issues in Ptolemaic/Roman overseas possessions. The date of minting is disputed.

28. Billon tetradrachm of Antoninus Pius (AD 138-161)

Diameter 23 mm
Weight 12.79 g
AD 159/160
Alexandria mint
CM.LS.2073-R

Obv. Laureate head of Antoninus Pius facing right. Accompanied by the Greek legend: ΑΝΤΩΝΙΝΟC-CEB EVCEB.

Rev. Isis Lactans seated on a throne facing right. The goddess wears a crown, which is now difficult to see. She also wears the Roman knotted garment. She holds her breast with her right hand to feed her young son, Harpocrates. He is supported by her left arm and wears the Crowns of Upper and Lower Egypt; in his left hand he holds a lotus flower.

In the field is the date L-Γ/K = year 23 Antoninus Pius' regnal dating.

SNG: pl. XLVII.2073

29 Basalt statue of a Ptolemaic queen

Height 42 cm
Ptolemaic period (first century BC)
Provenance unknown
Purchased
E.27.1981

Fragment of a full-length statue of a Ptolemaic queen, the head and bottom third are missing. There is further damage to the left hand.

This statue is a traditional Egyptian-style representation with a back pillar; the figure's left leg would have been placed forward giving the impression of striding forward. The subject is female, as indicated by the drapery and wig. The knotted garment and the double horn of plenty that the subject holds in her left arm identify her as a Ptolemaic queen. The *dikeras* or double horns are linked to only two queens, Arsinoe II, the sister and wife of Ptolemy II, who ruled with her brother from around 275-270 BC and Cleopatra VII, the last queen of the dynasty, who ruled from 51-30 BC (Ashton 2001: 41). Both queens use the double form of the symbol on coins (cat. 27) and in the case of Arsinoe II on inscribed representations. It is intended to represent fertility and typically overflows with the fruits of Egypt. It is Greek in origin. Similarly the locks of hair are not Egyptian, but first appear on representations of Libya, which was a Ptolemaic possession during the earlier history of the dynasty.

The knotted costume is thought to have been an adaptation of an older Egyptian style of knotted garment but here the layers of drapery are indicated in a manner commonly associated with Greek-style statuary (Bianchi 1980 and Ashton 2000). There are, however, earlier parallels for such drapery on painted wall reliefs, suggesting that the form of drapery here is not wholly outside the Egyptian repertoire.

It has been suggested that such statues represented the Ptolemaic queens as goddesses in their own right (Ashton 2000 and 2001). Many scholars associate this form of representation with the goddess Isis on account of later Roman adoption of the iconography to represent the goddess. However, inscribed statues representing Arsinoe II reveal no such affiliation.

In her right hand the deified queen holds a garland. This is the only example of such a statue being shown with this particular symbol, which suggests perhaps a funerary or festival association. The first century BC date is revealed by a stylistic comparison to others with these features, namely the length of hair, the style of drapery and the position of the proper right hand, which is usually clenched around an object in the usual Egyptian manner.

Vassilika 1995: 120-21 no. 56; Ashton 2000; 2001: 118-19 no. 67; 2003b: 115-52; Albersmeier 2002: 305-06 cat. No. 44 pl. 38.

Further reading: Ashton 2000 (including earlier bibliography).

30 Terracotta figure of Hathor-Aphrodite

Height 29.9 cm
Second to first century BC
Provenance unknown
Given by Mr and Mrs F.E. Brooks
E.6.1988

Nile silt clay. Mould-made in two halves. Traces of a plaster wash are preserved on the surface with further indications of red, grey and green-blue paint. The crown is broken, but the rest of the figure is preserved. There is an air hole at the back of the figure.

The figurine presents a naked woman adorned with jewellery. She wears a moulded necklace, a wrist bracelet on her proper right arm and the same, with an additional arm bracelet, on her left; across her right shoulder is a moulded breast chain, with a second indicated in red paint across the left shoulder. On her right ankle is another moulded band. On her head the subject wears a garland on top of which sits the crown of the goddesses Hathor and Isis, consisting of a sun disk and cow's horns.

The crown offers a clue to the identity of the figurine. Such images were often painted on the inside of coffins it is thought they were intended to represent 'Hathor of the West' who guided people to the next life, as a female equivalent to Osiris (Bailey in Walker and Higgs eds. 2001: 108-9, no. 137). Many scholars have associated the figures with the goddess Isis, the consort of Osiris, but given the strong funerary connections it would seem more likely that these figures represented Hathor. Part of the confusion seems to have been caused by the so-called Isis locks that form the coiffure of such figures. In fact this iconography was not adopted until the Roman period for this particular goddess, the Ptolemies continuing the tradition of the Late Period form of Isis (cat. 26). In addition to wearing the throne hieroglyph, Isis is often shown with the sun disk and cow's horn crown. Both goddesses wear the same crown in this period, although the sun disk and cow's horns were originally associated with Hathor.

This figurine doubtless served a funerary purpose and can perhaps be associated specifically with a female burial.

Further reading: Dunand 1990: 125-33 no. 327-349; Fjeldhagen 1995: 71-73 no. 50-52; Égypte Romaine 1997: 210-11 no. 217.

31 Terracotta figurine of Isis-Aphrodite

Height 22 cm
Second to third century AD
Provenance unknown, Egypt
E.P.358

Nile silt clay. Mould-made in two halves; the back is unmodelled. There are traces of a plaster wash on the amphora and drapery, with some traces also on the back. There are also iron stains on the back of the terracotta, which this figure has in common with several other unprovenanced pieces in the Fitzwilliam Museum, perhaps suggesting that they were excavated from the same area of a site (see also cat. 46). The figure is broken at the middle and had been repaired with a piece of wood inside and a plaster layer joining the two fragments and filling in the missing section. When the plaster and wood were removed it was revealed that this figure is in fact parts of two. The pair probably came from the same mould but there is a substantial difference in the thickness of the clay, indicating that the two pieces did not originally join.

The figure represented is female and in an undressed state. Her cloak has slipped from her shoulders onto her right leg in a manner more commonly associated with an Aphrodite type, the so-called Aphrodite of Melos, perhaps better known as the Venus di Milo type (Smith 1991: 80-81 fig. 305) Here, however, the garment is knotted, associating the subject with the goddess Isis. The inclusion of a vessel-a form associated with the transport of wine- to the main subject's left is a reference to festivals. The presence of the god Pan, who plays the double flutes, to the right also suggests a Bacchic celebration.

The nudity combined with the crown, which consists of a basket filled with fruit, might also suggest fertility. The basket also contains a *uraeus*, which by this period also appeared on representations of private individuals as well as members of the royal family and gods. The hands of the figure are raised to support the basket, which might be a link to the *Kanephoroi* or basket-bearers, a name given to the priestesses of Arsinoe II, whose cult continued well into the Roman period.

There are several known versions of this form of terracotta figure, which was obviously a common type. Its composition with links to well-known sculptures and iconographic forms suggest that it represented something quite specific. It is effectively an Egyptianised Aphrodite.

Compare: Dunand 1990: 180-182 no. 485-93; Fjeldhagen 1995: 117-21, no. 99-104.

32 Fragment of a terracotta figurine of Isis-Aphrodite

Height 12 cm
Dated by the excavator to circa AD 250.
House 'K' Ehnasya
Given by the Egypt Exploration Fund
E.126.1904

Nile silt clay. Only the upper section of this terracotta figure is preserved; it is broken and repaired at the neck. There are traces of plaster wash on the back of the figurine, but there are no visible traces of pigment preserved. The terracotta was mould-made in two separate halves and then joined. Only the back of the head appears to have been modelled at the rear.

The subject is female and wears a Greek *stephane* (crown) decorated with two garlands on either side. On top of the *stephane* is the Egyptian crown of the goddess Isis, consisting of a pair of cow's horns and a sun disk. The hair is rendered in a manner that was associated with the goddess Isis from the late first century AD, loosely styled at the top with locks falling onto the shoulders. On the right shoulder is the remains of a cloak that would have been tied in a knot between the breasts. This garment was also associated with the goddess Isis from the late first century AD.

It is possible that this terracotta formed part of either a full-length or a half figure. Both forms are common for this type of representation. This particular example is typical of the Roman period because it combines a Greek crown with an Egyptian headdress, perhaps suggesting that the figure was intended to represent Isis-Aphrodite rather than simply Isis, who more usually wears a festival garland rather than crown. It is also possible that whereas the Fitzwilliam Museum's terracotta represents the goddess herself, others wearing the garland are intended to be initiates of her cult.

House K at Ehnasya was excavated by Sir William Matthew Flinders Petrie in 1904. He speculated that the house had belonged to an iron-monger and noted coins dating to the third century AD, suggesting that the house could be dated to within ten years of AD 250. Several other terracotta figures were found there including 'Harpocrates, a seated nude, Aphrodite holding her hair, the goddess Ceres seated on a throne, girls seated on the ground and holding up their hands, an acrobat with a palm branch (cat. 86), a Roman comic actor, an ostrich..'. The Fitzwilliam Museum has other terracotta figures from this house that are not included in the exhibition (see on line catalogue).

Petrie 1905: 26-27, pl. XLVI.21.
Compare Dunand 1990: 148-57.

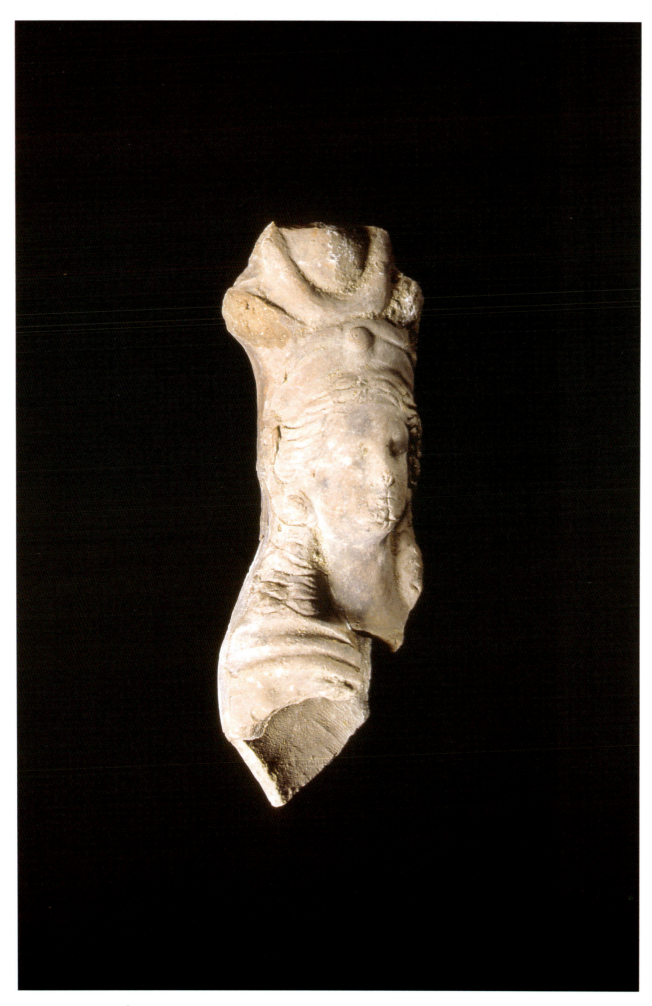

33. Copper alloy drachm of Faustina II

Diameter 33 mm
Weight 21.37 g
AD 148/149
Alexandria mint
CM.G.9-R

Obv. Bust of Faustina II (wife of Marcus Aurelius) facing right. Accompanied by the Greek legend: ΦΑVCTINA CEB-EVCEB CEB ΘVΓΑ.

Rev. Isis Pharia (of the Pharos) strides to the right and holds a sail that is blown by the wind in both hands and with her left foot. In her right hand she also holds an Egypitan rattle or sistrum. In front of the goddess is the Pharos (lighthouse), which is represented in the form of a square base and two further rounded levels. At the front is an entrance with steps and at the top is a statue of Zeus Soter surrounded by two Tritons blowing into a shell. Archaeologists believe that from the second century BC colossal Egyptian-style statues of Ptolemaic rulers stood in front of the famous lighthouse. Earthquakes finally destroyed the building and today Fort Quait Bey stands on what some believe to be the site of the ancient lighthouse. Ancient granite blocks have been incorporated into the medieval structure.

Around the edges is the date ΔΩΔΕΚΑΤΟ = year 12 of Marcus Aurelius' regnal dating.

Compare Milne 2010

34. Copper alloy diobol of Vespasian (AD 69-79)

Diameter 24 mm
Weight 6.51 g
AD 72/73
Alexandria mint
CM.G.3-R

Obv. A laureate portrait head of Vespasian facing right, accompanied by the Greek legend: [ΑVΤΟ]Κ ΚΑΙΣ ΣΕΒΑ ΟVΕΣΠΑΣΙΑΝΟV.

Rev. A bust of Isis facing right. The goddess wears a crown that is modelled on her Egyptian headdress of a sun-disk and cow's horns.

Representations of the goddess on lamps and statuary often show her with a crown of plumes; this form was a borrowing of a type of crown worn by Ptolemaic queens rather than the more traditional crown of Hathor and Isis that is shown on this Alexandrian coin.

In the right field is the date LE = year 5 of Vespasian's regnal dating.

Dattari 384

Osiris

35. Billon tetradrachm of Hadrian (AD 98-117)

Diameter 23.6 mm
Weight 12.91 g
AD 127/128
Alexandria mint
CM.G.6-R

Obv. Laureate, draped and cuirassed bust of Hadrian facing right and shown as if viewed from the back. Accompanied by the Greek legend: AVT [KAI]-TPAI AΔPIA CEB.

Rev. Ptah-Sokar-Osiris facing right. The god is represented in a mummified form and holds a sceptre with both hands. A statue similar to this figure was found at Hadrian's Villa outside Rome and represents the Memphite god Ptah.

Around the figure is the date L ΔΩΔE-KATOY = year 12 of Hadrian's regnal dating.

Milne 1259

36 Terracotta figure in the form of Osiris-Canopus

Height 15.0 cm
Second century AD
Provenance unknown
Bequeathed by E. Towry Whyte
E.268.1932

Nile silt clay, mould-made in two halves and then joined. There is some damage to the base of the figurine. Inside there are finger-marks where the maker has pushed the clay into a mould and there is an additional strip of clay on the inside right-hand side to reinforce the join. The surface is eroded and there are some cracks as a result of the firing process.

The jar is decorated with relief scenes. The lower registers contain two winged figures. On the front is a winged scarab wearing a sundisk and cow-horns. The beetle is probably a reference to re-birth in the after life and commonly appears on coffins. On the back of the jar is an eagle with the head turned to its right shoulder.

On the front of the jar, on a slightly higher register, are two figures of the child of Osiris and Isis: Harpocrates. The young child is depicted with finger in mouth and the side-lock of youth is just about distinguishable on the figure. Behind Harpocrates is a female figure holding a sceptre. She can probably be identified as Isis. The pectoral contains a figure of a seated deity who also appears to have the finger-to-mouth pose and who may also represent Harpocrates. Above this is a heart-shaped amulet, perhaps representing the heart of Osiris. The head of the figurine is human in form and shows the subject with a striated tripartite *nemes* headcloth. Unlike earlier representations of male gods there is no *uraeus* (protective cobra) shown.

Whilst such images may have served a funerary purpose because they are representations of Osiris, god of the afterlife, they certainly seem to have been used in temples and also in houses for personal shrines. It is not known whether they were developed in Egypt or Italy. Statues of priests holding an Osiris Canopus jar appear in both countries at around the same time in the first century AD. There are examples from the Sanctuary of Isis at Benevento (Müller 1971: : 23, 88-91 no. 284 pl. XXX) and also on the relief columns of the Iseum Campense in Rome (Lembke 1994: 186-89 pl. 5-8). In Egypt a basalt statue of a priest was found off the coastline of Alexandria (Dunand in Goddio et al. 1998: 189-94), accompanied by two Romano-Egyptian sphinxes, dating to the first century AD. Two large marble examples of Osiris-Canopus figures were found at a temple dedicated to Isis at Ras el-Soda in Alexandria, and are displayed in the Greco-Roman Museum. These figures were also popular in Italy, where they were often carved from hard Egyptian stones in order to evoke their eastern origins. There are several now housed in the Vatican Museums (Botti and Romanelli 1951: 122-24 no. 199-202 pl. LXXXIV).

Jars with the head of Isis were also manufactured (Bianchi in Bianchi ed. 1988: 248-9 no. 136) and appear with Osiris Canopus on coinage (cat. 37).

Compare: Dunand 1990: 158-61 no. 426-436; Fjeldhagen 1995: 77 no. 56.

37. Copper alloy drachm of Hadrian (AD 117-138)

Diameter 31 mm
Weight 17.19g
AD 133/134
Alexandria mint
CM.G.8-R

Obv. Laureate, draped and cuirassed bust of Hadrian facing right and shown as if viewed from the back. Accompanied by the Greek legend: AVT KAIC TPAIAN-AΔPIANO[C CEB].

Rev. Di-style Egyptian temple with papyrus columns and rounded pediment which displays a sun-disk and *uraei*; within the temple are two facing canopic jars with the heads of Isis (left) and Osiris (right). Two large marble statues of Osiris-Canopus were recovered from the Hadrianic temple of Isis at Ras el-Soda in eastern Alexandria. It is likely that this coin represents a similar temple within the city.

In the field is the date L-IH = year 18 of Hadrian's regnal dating.

Milne 1431

38. Billon tetradrachm of Gallienus (AD 253-268)

Diameter 24 mm
Weight 11.19 g
261/262
Alexandria mint
CM.LS.2088-R

Obv. Laureate and cuirassed bust of Gallienus shown as if viewed from the front. Accompanied by the Greek legend: AYT K Π ΛIK ΓAΛΛIHNOC CEB.

Rev. Osiris-Canopus wearing an atef crown. The body is decorated with two standing figures, probably Harpocrates.

In the field is the date: L-Θ = year 9 of Gallianus' regnal dating.

SNG: XLVIII.2088

Serapis

39 Steatite statuette of Serapis wearing a toga

Height 7.5 cm
First century AD
Provenance unknown, probably Egypt
Purchased from Sir William Matthew Flinders Petrie
E.87.1900

This small statuette shows a bearded male deity. The subject's left arm is missing and the right arm is preserved to the elbow. The legs and feet are also missing. There is a drill hole at the top of the head, which originally supported a crown. There is also a second hole for the left arm, which might suggest that it was raised upwards, perhaps holding onto a sceptre; this would have been more easily slotted into a socket to allow for the positioning of the arm.

The thick beard and hair are arranged in a series of stylised curls. The subject also wears a Roman toga, which places it firmly within the Roman period. The features listed above represented several Roman deities, namely Jupiter, Neptune, Ammon and Zeus-Ammon. However, the drill hole at the top of the head suggests that a small crown was inserted, a feature associated with Serapis. It is possible that the crown took one of two forms: either a *modius* or a group of lotus leaves (Rausch ed. 1998: 244 no. 181 where it is correctly dated to the first century AD; it is possible that it is even second century). The latter feature is common during the reign of the Emperor Hadrian, when it replaces many traditional motifs on statues representing Egyptian deities. The thick rendering of the hair and beard might also reflect Imperial fashions of the early- mid second century AD, when Hadrian ruled.

During the Roman period many Egyptian gods adopted the toga, even those represented in Egypt. Key deities who were associated with the Imperial house often wore the cuirass and Bes, who was popular with the Roman soldiers, can be found in a Roman military uniform (Cat. 59 and Bianchi in Bianchi ed. 1988: 208 no. 102; Égypte Romaine 1997: 228-33 no. 248-54).

Steatite was a common medium for small-scale statuettes and vessels between the first century BC and the second AD. Although its appearance is that of a hard stone it is relatively soft and so easier to carve and perhaps for this reason it was popular with Roman artists.

Further reading: Ashton 2003: 10-14; Ashton in Hirst and Silk eds. 2004: 22-25.

40 Fragment of a terracotta figure of Serapis

Height 8 cm
First to Second century AD
Ehnasya
Given by the Egypt Exploration Fund
E.125.1904

Nile silt clay, mould-made in two parts and joined together; there is a clear line down the sides of the figure. There are traces of plaster wash on the surface of the terracotta. The top of the headdress has been cut and placed on top of the figure to seal it.

The figure is a bearded male who can be identified as Serapis by the *modius* or grain measure on his head, which is decorated with foliage at the front. The fringe is parted down the centre with two waves of hair in opposite directions and the beard is only just parted into two. These two features suggest that this is an earlier representation of the god, still dating to the Roman period, but perhaps soon after the adoption of the grain measure as part of the Serapis repertoire. It is likely that this figure represented a standing Serapis type, as was more commonly depicted on forms with a moulded back. Seated representations are usually more two-dimensional with a flatter, un-modelled back.

Petrie 1905: pl. XLVI no. 18, with no house reference.

41. Billon tetradrachm of Antoninus Pius (AD 138-161)

Diameter 24 mm
Weight 12.65 g
AD 143/144
Alexandria mint
CM.LS.2069-R

Obv. Laureate head of Antoninus Pius facing right. Accompanied by the Greek legend: ΑΝΤΩΝΙΝΟC-CEB EYCEB.

Rev. A seated representation of Serapis wearing a *modius* (grain measure). The god sits on a throne facing left, holding a sceptre in his left hand and reaching out towards the three-headed god Cerberus with his right.

In the field is the date L-Z = year 7 of Antoninus Pius' regnal dating.

SNG: pl.XLVII.2069

42. Copper alloy drachm of Lucius Verus (AD 161-169)

Diameter 35 mm
Weight 23.22 g
AD 166/167
Alexandria mint
CM.664-1948

Obv. Laureate, draped and cuirassed bust of Lucius Verus facing right and seen as if viewed from the back. Accompanied by the Greek legend: Λ ΑVPHΛIOC-OVHPOC CEB.

Rev. A standing figure of Serapis facing left. The god wears a garment draped around his waist and is crowned with the *modius*. In his right hand he holds a *taenia* (fillet) and in his left a cornucopia.

This standing form of Serapis (earlier Sarapis) is believed to represent the god's statue at Memphis, and the seated version to be the Alexandrian cult statue. This suggestion is questionable (cat. 19) and it is possible that the seated Serapis was a Roman development.

In the field is the date L-Z = year 7 of Lucius Verus' regnal dating.

Harpocrates

43. Copper alloy drachm of Trajan (AD 98-117)

Diameter 35 mm
Weight 19.88 g
AD 109/110
Alexandria mint
CM.46-1934

Obv. Laureate and draped bust of the Emperor Trajan facing right. Accompanied by the Greek legend: AVT TPAIAN CE-B ΓEP[M ΔAKIK].

Rev. A figure of the god Harpocrates, who can be identified by the Crowns of Upper and Lower Egypt, the cornucopia in his proper left arm and the finger-to-mouth gesture. The young god sits on a human-headed sphinx and turns to the left. Beneath the sphinx are lotus flowers, perhaps referring to fertility and the flooding of the Nile.

The sphinx became an important emblem of Egypt; pairs of sphinxes commonly appeared on Roman wall paintings of Egyptian sanctuaries in order to invoke the province. Harpocrates is perhaps an unusual choice for a god but his figurines were made in large numbers in Egypt, where he was popular throughout the Roman period (cats. 44-49).

In the field is the date LI-Γ = year 13 of Trajan's regnal dating.

BMC 460

44 Terracotta figure of Harpocrates wearing an Egyptian crown and headdress
(left)

Height 22.5 cm
Second to Third centuries AD
House 'N', Ehnasya
Given by the Egypt Exploration Fund
E.127.1904

Nile silt clay, mould-made in two halves; the back is unmodelled. The surface is covered in deposits of soluble salts. The figure stands on a hollow, asymmetrical base.

The image represents the young Horus or Harpocrates as he was known to the classical world. He can be identified by the finger-to-mouth pose, which is Egyptian in origin and also the hm.hm.t crown and *nemes* headcloth, both features are found on Egyptian-style representations of the god. In his left hand he appears to hold a club, which associates him with the god Hercules. This was a Ptolemaic addition, which appears most commonly in the Roman period. It is thought to be a rather tenuous link to the birth place of Harsomtous, who was the brother of Harpocrates. Harsomtous was born in the town of Herakleopolis, literally the city of Hercules (Török 1995: 77). Both child gods were also believed to have been born out of a lotus flower.

The pose adopted by Harpocrates on this particular figure is also influenced by the classical tradition; he is shown as a plump child with a rounded face, wearing a long diaphanous dress. His stance is relaxed with the weight evenly distributed onto his bare feet. A column, a common feature on Romano-Egyptian terracotta figurines, supports his left arm. The style of the *nemes* headcloth, with its thin lappets and lack of *uraeus*, is typical of figures of the second and third centuries AD.

Harpocrates was the Greek and Roman version of the young Horus and one of the few Egyptian gods to be adopted into the Ptolemaic Greek repertoire. In this capacity he was no longer shown as a small adult, as in Egyptian art, but as a young chubby child. In many respects his image was the same as that of Eros. The only difference between the two is that Eros is shown with wings. The iconography of Harpocrates changed during the Roman period and was by no means static, as seen by the variety of figurines illustrated in this catalogue. As the young Horus, Harpocrates was the son of Isis and Osiris, but the association became much wider in the Roman period and the god often appeared in festival guise or with a club as here, associating him with a specific city. Indeed it is possible that such figurines were intended to represent Harsomtous.

Petrie (1905: 27) suggested that those figures of Harpocrates with Egyptian features were earlier in date than those inspired by the classical tradition. However, purely Greek-style figures of Harpocrates were manufactured in the Ptolemaic period and it is likely that both Greek and Egyptian versions survived into the Roman period and continued to be made. In his publication of the piece Petrie mentioned that House N at Ehnasya contained similar figures to the aforementioned house K (1905: 27).

Petrie 1905: 27 pl. XLVI no. 30.

45 Terracotta figure of Harpocrates wearing the Crown of Upper and Lower Egypt
(middle)

Height 20 cm
Dated by the excavator to the fourth century AD
House 'H' Ehnasya
Given by the Egypt Exploration Fund
E.119.1904

Nile silt clay, mould-made in two halves. There are traces of plaster on the back and the surface is stained black in places. The head is repaired and part of the right hand side is missing. The back is well modelled and rather than standing on the usual base the figure has fully modelled legs and feet.

The figure wears a diaphanous dress to the knees and stands barefoot. In his left hand is a club associating him with Hercules; the right index finger is raised to the mouth. On his head is a small version of the Crowns of Upper and Lower Egypt, decorated with two ears of corn and a piece of fruit.

The figure is shown with a paunch and a rounded childlike face: the side lock on the right-hand side also indicates the youthfulness of the god and suggests he is Harpocrates.

Petrie 1905: 27.
Compare Fjeldhagen 1995: 38 no. 14, which is dated to the first century AD and Dunand 1990: 76-77 no. 148-51.

46 Terracotta figure of Harpocrates with jar and festival crown
(right)

Height 23.9 cm
First to second centuries AD
Provenance unknown, Egypt
E.P. 357

Nile silt clay, mould-made in two halves. The back is roughly modelled and there are iron corrosion products impregnated in the surface of the area around the buttocks and back, similar to those visible on cat. 31 suggesting that the two came from the same site or were deposited in the same conditions. There are black stains on the surface and possible black pigment on the side-lock with traces of pink on the base and on the crown. There are traces of plaster wash on the surface, which would have acted as a base for the painted decoration. The figure stands on a rounded, hollow base.

The figure is naked and stands with his weight on his right leg in a relaxed position. He holds a jar in his left hand and his right index finger is raised to his mouth in the usual fashion. On his head he wears a festival crown with two ears of corn. The side-lock is just visible on the right side of his head. A moulded bracelet is worn on the right wrist. Harpocrates with a jar appeared in the Ptolemaic period: the jar has been seen as a reference to festivals, an interpretation supported here by the festival crown.

Compare Petrie 1905: pl. XLVII no. 38; Fjeldhagen 1995: 34, no. 9; Dunand 1990: 72-73 no. 134-140.

47 Terracotta figure of Harpocrates riding a cockerel (left)

Height 14.5 cm
First century AD
Provenance unknown
Given by R.G. Gayer-Anderson
E.GA.2934.1943

Fine Nile silt clay, mould-made in two halves and modelled on both sides. There is an air hole at the rear to improve circulation during firing. There are traces of a plaster wash on the beak of the bird. The tail is broken and repaired with modern plaster. There is red pigment on the crest and the wattle of the cockerel, the legs, arms and cloak of the rider.

The main figure is a cockerel, which carries a small figure on its back. The head of the rider is missing, but enough survives to indicate that it was a child wearing a cloak. Since the figure is child-like in appearance and this is a known Harpocrates type, we can assume that this figurine represented the god. The same young deity is also depicted on the back of a duck, or riding a variety of different animals. This practice may have originated from the similarity of his appearance to that of the baby Dionysos who often rides exotic beasts as a reminder of his Indian ancestry.

Compare: Fjeldhagen (1995) 43-44, no. 20; Török 76-77, no. 84 and no. 85; Égypte Romaine 1997: 220-21 no. 235.

Further reading: Ashton 2003: 78-80.

48 Terracotta figure of Harpocrates riding a horse (middle)

Height 13.1 cm
First to second centuries AD
Naukratis
Given by the British School of Archaeology in Egypt
E.233.1899

Coarse over-fired Nile silt clay, mould-made in two halves and joined. There are traces of a plaster wash and possibly black pigment on the front of the figure. There is an air hole at the rear, which has been pushed out at the back as indicated by the edges of the clay. The base is oval in form and supports the feet of the horse. The surface is spalled and pitted.

This figurine and the next show two different forms of child riding a horse. Here the small child appears in the finger-to-mouth pose and wearing a festival crown, with two ears of corn protruding from the top of what is presumably a garland. The front leg of the horse is raised in a manner found on terracotta figurines dating to the Ptolemaic period and showing a Macedonian rider, presumed to be one of the Ptolemies. The method of manufacture, with an unmodelled flat back, is more typical of the Roman period (Ashton 2003: 78-79).

Compare: Dunand 1990: 83-84 no. 168-174; Fjeldhagen (1995) 45-49, no's. 21-24.

49 Terracotta figure of a horseman wearing a hooded garment (right)

Height 13.7 cm
Second to third centuries AD
Antinoe (?)
Given by the Egypt Exploration Fund
E.108.1914

Coarse Nile silt clay, mould-made in two halves and joined. The combined front and back feet of the horse form the base of this figurine. There are patches of abrasion covering the surface.

The schematic form of the horse suggests a date later in the Roman period than those previously discussed. There is a substantial hole through the nose of the horse, but there is no sign of corrosion products or wear. It is possible to see the direction in which the clay was pushed through the hole. This feature appears on other terracotta representations dating to the third century and later.

The rider turns to his right, towards the viewer. He wears a hooded cloak and appears to have had a rounded, child-like face. He holds on to the horse's mane with his hands. At the rear it is just possible to make out the rider's other leg and also the round boss of a shield. This form of terracotta is similar to Persian period representations of Scythian riders. Here, however, in a Romano-Egyptian context it seems likely that the rider is a child god.

Compare Petrie 1905: pl. XLVIII no. 53-54, which show youthful male figures, the latter holding his finger to his mouth (54 = UC 50594 Petrie Museum of Egyptian Archaeology, London); Fjeldhagen 1995: 48-49 no. 24.

50. Copper alloy drachm of Hadrian (AD II7-I38)

Diameter 30 mm
Weight 19.52 g
AD 133/134
Alexandria mint
CM.LS.2063-R

Obv. Laureate, draped and cuirassed bust of Hadrian, shown as if viewed from the back. Accompanied by the Greek legend: AVT KAIC TPAIAN-AΛPIANOC CEB.

Rev. Facing busts of Serapis (left wearing a *modius*) and Isis (right wearing a sun-disk, cow's horn and double plume crown); in between the two deities is the standing figure of Harpocrates, wearing the Dual Crown, holding a cornucopia in his left hand and raising his right index finger to his mouth. Below is an eagle with spread wings. Here Serapis replaces Osiris, the traditional father of the young Horus. By the Roman period, both Isis and Serapis had become internationally popular and regular consorts.

Low in the field is the date L-IH = year 18 of Hadrian's regnal dating.

SNG: pl. XLVII.2063

5I. Copper alloy obol of Domitian (AD 8I-96)

Diameter 20 mm
Weight 3.88 g
AD 86/87
Alexandria mint
CM.G.4-R

Obv. Laureate head of Domitian facing right, accompanied by the Greek legend: [AVT] KAIΣAP ΔOMITIANOΣ ΣEB ΓE[PM]. In the field is the date Lϛ = year 6 of Domitian's regnal dating.

Rev. A Hawk facing right and crowned with a lotus or perhaps the Dual Crown of Upper and Lower Egypt. The hawk represented the god Horus with whom the king of Egypt was associated.

RPC II, 2533

52. Copper alloy drachm of Hadrian (AD 117-138)

Diameter 34 mm
Weight 25.55 g
AD 134/135
Alexandria mint
CM.677-1948

Obv. Laureate, draped and cuirassed bust of Hadrian, shown as if viewed from the back. Accompanied by the Greek legend: [AVT] KAIC TPAIAN-[AΔPIANOC CEB].

Rev. Harpocrates holding a club stands to the left and in front of an altar in the form of a lotus pillar. This particular form of the god is associated with the city of Herakleopolis in Middle Egypt. The young god is dressed in a long robe similar to the Greek *peplos* and is crowned with lotus or schematic form of the Crowns of Upper and Lower Egypt. In his left hand he holds a club and brings index finger of his right hand close to his mouth.

In the field is the date LENN-EAKΔ = year 19 of Hadrian's regnal dating.

Milne 1471

Zeus Ammon

53 Copper alloy weight in the form of Zeus Ammon

Height 6.6 cm
Second to Third centuries AD
Provenance unknown
E.GA.2840.1943

Cast copper alloy figure made by the lost wax casting technique with traces of lead at the back, including a substantial lump of the metal. The neck and back of the loop are roughly finished due to poor modelling. It is possible that the lead was inserted into and joined to the back in order to increase the weight of the piece.

The Greeks had worshipped Zeus Ammon, and the Romans simply adopted the god's Greek iconography, that of a bearded male with ram's horns attached to the sides of the head. The head on this weight also wears a *modius* (grain measure), more usually attributed to Serapis (cat. 40). The hook to support the weight is conveniently attached to the back. The head differs from that of Zeus or Serapis in that the beard is not parted into two and the fringe does not consist of ringlets.

Zeus Ammon was closely associated with Alexander the Great, who visited the Oracle of Ammon at Siwa in 332 BC. Alexander marched his army across the desert for a journey that today takes around seven hours by road from Alexandria. Alexander, we are told was seized by a *pothos* (desire) to visit the oracle, famed throughout the Greek world. Some literary sources report that Alexander was there declared the son of Ammon (Egyptian Amun who was equivalent to Zeus). As was the case with its adoption of many Egyptian gods the classical world felt a need to define their roles or forms more specifically. Hence Zeus-Amun became a hybrid god.

Further reading: Égypte Romaine 1997: 260-61 no. 293.

54. Copper alloy drachm of Antoninus Pius (AD 138-161)

Diameter 33 mm
Weight 20.71 g
AD 151/152
Alexandria mint
CM.G.10-R

Obv. Laureate head of Antoninus Pius facing left. Accompanied by the Greek legend: ΑΥΤ Κ Τ Α[ΙΛ ΑΔΡ-ΑΝΤΩΝΙΝ]ΟC-CEB EVC.

Rev. Bust of Ammon or Zeus Ammon facing right. Below the god is a ram, also facing right.

In the field is a date L-[I]E = year 15 of Antoninus Pius' regnal dating.

Milne 2153

Agathos Daimon

55. Billon tetradrachm of Hadrian (AD 117-138)

Diameter 23.6 mm
Weight 13.45 g
AD 117/118
Alexandria mint
CM.57-1943

Obv. Laureate bust of Hadrian facing right, with drapery on his left shoulder. Accompanied by the Greek legend: [A]VT KAI-T-PIANOC (*sic*)-[...]

Rev. Agathos Daemon wearing the Dual Crowns of Upper and Lower Egypt. The tail is curled around and supports the rearing snake. To the left is a *caduceus*, a symbol associated with the god Hermes/Mercury.

In the field is the date **L-B** = year 2 of Hadrian's regnal dating.

Milne 837

56. Billon tetradrachm of Hadrian (AD 117-138)

Diameter 23.2 mm
Weight 13.28 g
AD 125/126
Alexandria mint
CM.28.1206-1920

Obv. Laureate, draped and cuirassed bust of Hadrian, facing right and shown as if viewed from the back. Accompanied by the Greek legend: AVT KAI-TPAI AΔPIA CEB.

Rev. On the left is Agathos Daimon who faces a *uraeus* (cobra) on the right. Between the two gods is a club and in the left field a *caduceus*. Agathos Daimon represented the good spirit while the *uraeus* represented the eye of the sun god Ra and is most commonly found on the headdresses of members of the royal family or gods.

Around the two snakes is the date **L ΔE-KA-TOY** = year 10 of Hadrian's regnal dating.

Milne 1166

Composite Deities

57 Re-used limestone stela showing the gods Isis, Horus, Tutu and Helios

Height 33.3 cm
First to third centuries AD
Provenance unknown, Egypt
Given by the British School of Archaeology in Egypt
E.10.1922

Only the upper section of this limestone stela is preserved, the lower section including the text is missing. There are visible fault lines in the stone. There are traces of black pigment on the surface, which is from the original painted stela. The base line can clearly be seen, with a second line visible roughly half way down the stela. In the right corner, close to the replacement that is now carved, are the remains of a bird wing, and two standing figures.

At the top, carved in low relief, is a winged sun-disk and two cobras. The main scene shows, from the viewer's left, the god Helios, identified by the crown of sun rays that he wears; the god Tutu in the form of a sphinx; and a female deity with a snake body, who has been identified as Isis in the form of a serpent, but is probably more specifically Isis Thermouthis (Frankfurter 1998: 39-40 and cat. 58).

The stela shows a combination of Egyptian and foreign traditions. The form of altar, on which Isis Thermouthis sits, appears on Greek-style vases dating to the Ptolemaic period and the form that the goddess takes is reminiscent of Romano-Egyptian terracotta figurines. Tutu, however, is wholly Egyptian in execution. The god appears as a striding sphinx wearing the *atef* crown, which is decorated with two cobras. Helios stands uncomfortably with his right arm awkwardly twisted in order to hold the staff or sceptre placed behind him. This exact pose appears on a Ptolemaic stela now in the Royal Ontario Museum, Toronto showing Arsinoe II standing in front of an altar; her arm is positioned in the same way and it has been suggested that this was an attempt by the Egyptian artist to render a more naturalistic or Greek stance. Helios' face looks straight at the viewer, the torso is twisted in a three-quarter view and his feet are in profile. It seems likely that this scene was carved by an Egyptian artist who was attempting to copy a Greek model. It is also possible that the accompanying text was in Greek.

Martin forthcoming
Further Reading: Frankfurter 1998: 115-16.

95

58 Copper alloy fitting: Isis and Dionysos

Height 13.8 cm
First century AD
Provenance unknown
Corpus Christi College Loan Ant. 103.364

Solid cast copper alloy fitting in the form of two serpents with entwined tails. The tails are broken and only partially preserved. There is a modern pin at the back of the piece and it is uncertain whether there was one in this position. There is a notable depression in the surrounding area around this hole and it would also appear that the hole, if indeed there was originally this feature, has been expanded to accommodate the pin. There are traces of investment material that was trapped at the back of the tails after casting the piece, suggesting that this part was not on display. There are also two short sections at the back of the snakes which again suggests the piece was inserted into another object.

The serpent on the viewer's right has a male, bearded head, crowned with a corn-measure. Although this motif was associated primarily with Serapis, other gods such as Zeus Ammon may also wear it as a reference to fertility. The long pointed beard on this particular representation, however, is suggestive of the god Dionysos, or more specifically Dionysos Sardanapollos.

The female serpent, on the left, wears a crown consisting of two plumes, elongated cow's horns and a sun disk. This headdress was traditionally closely associated with the goddess Hathor. Unlike Hathor, however, this female figure wears her hair in locks and so can be associated with Isis. Terracotta figurines and depictions of Isis on oil lamps show that she was commonly shown with this crown and hairstyle from the first century AD onwards. Here she may represent Isis Thermouthis, who was known as Renenutet in the New Kingdom (Fjeldhagen 1995: 66-67 no. 44-45). Isis-Thermouthis was an agricultural goddess. Both snakes have scales and a softer underbelly and the eyes of both Dionysos and Isis are made from three simple holes. It is not clear whether this feature was cast or whether the holes were simply punched later.

Snakes were a popular aspect of Romano-Egyptian figurines. They appear not only in the form of the traditional *uraeus* but also as the god *agathos daimon*, or the good spirit/demon. Alexander the Great was closely linked to this god and snakes appear frequently in the literature to save or guide the ruler. It is said that during the laying out of the foundations of Alexandria Alexander was perturbed by the presence of a snake. When he ordered it to be killed many more appeared from the spot and dispersed throughout the city. This was interpreted as a good omen. Similarly when Alexander marched his men across the desert to the temple of Ammon at Siwa Oasis, in one version of the story a snake appeared to guide him. The protective and guiding roles attributed to the snakes thus led to their protective role and the adoption of their form by several gods. Such images also often frequently appear in funerary contexts.

Compare the grave stelae: Égypte Romaine 1997: 204-05 no. 207; Ashton and Higgs in Walker and Higgs 2001: 124-25 no. 151.

Bes and Beset

59 Terracotta figure showing Bes as a soldier

Height 21 cm
First to second centuries AD
Provenance unknown, Egypt
Bequeathed by E. Towry Whyte
E.207.1932

Nile silt clay, mould-made in three parts: the front, which was pushed into a mould and sealed with a flat clay back, the shield and the base, which is also sealed at the top. The back of the piece is not modelled but there are the remains of four points of clay which indicate that the figure was fired on its back and was propped during this process on account of the depth of the base. There are traces of a plaster wash on the surface.

Bes is always shown as a dwarf-like figure with leonine ears and ruff. His face is exaggerated, with mask-like features and he usually extends his tongue. Traditionally, he was a household deity who protected sleepers, women in childbirth and women from each other's jealousy. In the Roman period, however, he became associated with new and more specific social groups in society.

Here we see Bes as a Roman soldier. He wears a tunic and skirt that is moulded in a fashion to suggest that it is made from a series of tongues. In his left hand he holds an oval shield. His right arm is raised and holds a small sword or dagger towards his crown. The headdress is made up of five plumes in the traditional form for Bes. His tongue is not obviously projecting, but the surface in this area is rather worn.

Bes appears with a sword in the Ptolemaic period but he usually stands with only a panther skin and is not dressed in military attire. He became enormously popular with Roman troops in Egypt. Although no temples were dedicated specifically to him, he remained popular as a household deity and his statue was often included in temples to other gods. A figure similar to this, but dating to the Ptolemaic period, was found as a dedication within a wall at Athribis (Szymanska and Babraj 2004: 4), thus stressing the potency of the god's powers. Only the sword indicates his warrior status in the Ptolemaic period; Roman examples show him in full military dress.

Compare: Fjeldhagen 1995: 78 no. 57; Égypte Romaine 1997: 224 no. 240.

Further reading: Frankfurter 1998: 125-31.

60 Copper alloy fitting in the form of Beset

Height 7.4 cm
First to second centuries AD
Tanis, perhaps
Given by Revd. A.B. Cheales
E.3.1853

Hollow cast copper alloy fitting or attachment in the form of the goddess Beset. The figure was cast open at the back and there are the remains of the core from casting. There are cracks at the lower edges of the piece, beneath the breasts; this feature is the result of casting flaws during firing. There is some damage to the crown but the figure is otherwise intact.

Bes did not traditionally have a consort, but in the late Ptolemaic or early Roman period a female version was frequently found at his side. Her name was Beset (the feminine form of Bes in Egyptian, where a .t is added). Like Bes, Beset was a dwarf and many of her features echoed those of her consort. She wears the same crown as Bes, consisting of five plumes, and her face has very similar features on a more feminine scale. It has been suggested that there are examples of a female Bes dating to the New Kingdom (Bosse-Griffiths 2001), these, however, are rare.

Her costume is not always consistent, but interestingly she often wears a knotted dress and can be seen here with her hair styled in a way more typically associated with Isis. The breasts are also prominent on this particular example. All of these features suggest that the subject is associated in some way with one of the roles of Isis herself. Since Bes was connected to childbirth and the protection of pregnant women, it is easy to see how his consort could take on a similar role. The pair are sometimes shown with little Bes children, tiny versions of their parents (see Fjeldhagen 1995: 82-83 no. 62-63).

Nilus

61. Billon tetradrachm of Trajan (AD 98-117)

Diameter 23.8 mm
Weight 11.53 g
AD 115/6
Alexandria mint
CM.50-1943

Obv. Laureate head of Trajan, facing right. Accompanied by the Greek legend: AVT TPAIAN APICEB ΓEPM ΔAKIK. In front of the Emperor is a star.

Rev. Bust of Nilus facing right. The god can be identified by his beard and the crown of lotus buds. Behind him is a cornucopia, representing fertility and the flooding of the river Nile.

In the field is the date LI-Θ = year 19 of Trajan's regnal dating.

Compare Milne 728

62. Copper alloy drachm of Antoninus Pius (AD 138-161)

Diameter 33 mm
Weight 23.30
AD 144/145
Alexandria mint
CM.84-1934

Obv. Laureate head of Antoninus Pius facing right, accompanied by the Greek legend: AVT K T AIΛ AΔP-ANTΩNE[INOC] CEB EVC.

Rev. Bust of Nilus facing right. The god can be identified by the lotus crown and the two accompanying fish. Behind the god, to the left, is a sceptre. In the field to the right is a star, and the date L-H = year 8 of Antoninus Pius' regnal dating.

Compare Milne 1825

63. Billon tetradrachm of Hadrian (AD 117-138)

Diameter 25 mm
Weight 12.86 g
AD 132/133
Alexandria mint
CM.LS.2058-R

Obv. A laureate, draped and cuirassed bust of Hadrian, facing right and shown as if viewed from the back. Accompanied by the Greek legend: AVT KAIC–TPAI AΔPIA CEB.

Rev. The god Nilus reclines facing left. A garment is partly draped around his lower abdomen and legs. He wears a crown of lotus buds, and holds a reed or a branch of corn in his right hand and cornucopia in the left. To the right is a crocodile.

In the left field is the date: LIZ = year 17 of Hadrian's regnal dating.

SNG.pl.XLVII.2058

103

64. Copper alloy sestertius of Hadrian (AD 117-138)

Diameter 33 mm
Weight 27.33 g
AD 119-138
Rome mint
CM.1546-1963

Obv. Laureate and draped bust of Hadrian, accompanied by the Latin legend: HADRIANVS-AVG COS III P P.

Rev. The god faces right, and is accompanied by his name is Latin above and S C in exergue. Nilus is naked to the waist, and reclines on what appears to be a rock. He holds a reed in his right hand and cornucopia in his left, with which play two children. To the right is a hippopotamus; and above it are reeds; below the god is a crocodile.

Nilus was a popular god in Rome and appears in a sculptured form on a number of occasions. He is also often accompanied by statues of crocodiles stressing his Egyptian origin and allowing the viewer to differentiate between him and other river gods. As is usual on coins minted in Rome, the god is labelled. Several statues of the god have been found in Italy (Botti and Romanelli 1951: 115-18 no. 183-84 no. 186-87 pl. LXXXIX).

RIC II, 863

Romano-Egyptian material culture

Vessels

65 Oil lamp showing the goddess Isis

Height 2.8 cm Length 7.8 cm
AD 150-250
Provenance unknown
Given by Revd. Greville John Chester
GR.15h.1891

The lamp is mould-made in two halves in silty, probably Egyptian, clay but copies an imported Italian form. The lamp has a heart-shaped nozzle, and the oil hole is off-centre to the viewer's left. The base and sides have become misshapen during firing and as a consequence the lamp does not sit flat on a surface. It is likely, however, that it was still functional and is therefore not technically a waster. The discus is confined within two concentric circles and the handle is ribbed. It is covered in a red-brown glaze. There is a small air hole to the left of the central oil hole and a second marked but not pierced hole above this.

The discus is decorated with a bust of the goddess Isis, distinguished by her knotted costume, corkscrew locks and crown. All of these features can be traced back to representations of Ptolemaic queens in the third to first centuries BC (cat. 29); however, they are adopted during the reign of Domitian to represent the goddess Isis.

The crown that is represented on this Roman lamp is also of a type associated with Egyptian royal women, consisting of double plumes, a sun disk and cow's horns. Isis in Egypt is typically shown with either a throne sign or the sun disk and cow's horns (a crown originally worn by Hathor and with whom Isis became assimilated). Underneath the bust of Isis is a bird with outstretched wings, almost certainly an eagle.

Compare Bailey 1988: Q2036, 249 pl. 43.
Further Reading: Podvin 2002: 243-48 and 357-76.

66 Oil lamp showing the god Serapis

Height 3.3 cm Length 8.0 cm
AD 150-250
Provenance unknown
Given by Revd. Greville John Chester
GR.15c.1891

The lamp has been over-fired and as a consequence the glaze is uneven and very thick in places. The handle and discus are decorated with a ribbed design, and the oil hole is positioned off-centre, to the viewer's left. There appears to be a maker's mark on the base but this is obscured by the glaze.

Copy of an Italian form in Nile silt clay showing the seated Serapis with a sceptre in his left hand and the three-headed dog Cerberus at his feet, to the viewer's left. The god wears a *modius* and is seated on a throne, the back of which is visible. This type of Serapis is the same as that shown in cat. 19.

Compare: Bailey 1988: Q2040, 249 pl. 43.

67 Oil lamp showing the god Osiris

Height 3.5 cm Length 8.1 cm
AD 150-250
Provenance unknown
Given by Revd. Greville John Chester
GR.15d.1891

The lamp has an off-centre oil hole, damaged around the edges. There is further damage to the underside of the lamp on account of the thin clay. The bottom is decorated with a maker's mark in the form of a schematic ear of corn. The base of the nozzle is decorated with three raised dots, and there are two concentric ridges surrounding the image of Osiris on the discus, with a ribbed handle at the top. There are traces of a red slip on the surface of the lamp with discoloration from over-firing. The clay is of a dark silty type with large lime inclusions.

This oil lamp is a copy of an imported Italian form that was also produced in Egypt. Rather than showing either Osiris in the Canopic form or the hybrid god Serapis, a bust of the Egyptian style of Osiris decorates the discus. The god can be identified by his mummified form, the *atef* crown and the crook and flail that he holds across his chest. Although the god still appears in this form in Egypt, there are only a handful of examples showing him in this guise from Italy, mostly dating from the second and third centuries AD.

68 Terracotta lamp holder in the form of Harpocrates

Height 15 cm
Second century AD
Provenance unknown
Given by R.G. Gayer-Anderson
E.GA.2930.1943

A complete lamp holder made from Nile silt clay and with traces of white plaster wash on the surface. Some discoloration to the clay has occurred, resulting in a yellow tinge. This is caused by iron corrosion products on the surface, probably the result of the object lying in proximity to corroding iron.

The front of the head and lower main section is mould-made; the back is hand-modelled. There is a square hole at the rear to allow a miniature lamp to be inserted and the front lower section is decorated with a lozenge-shaped lattice that has been cut from strips of clay, to allow the light to escape.

The head (hollow in form) is that of a young boy, who wears a *uraeus* (cobra) but who is without the usual side-lock of a child. The top of the head is modelled into a device for hanging the holder, and there is a small hole pierced through the top. A miniature lamp would have been placed in the back of the holder and would have lit up the lower section. It is likely that this object served a ritual purpose as part of a household shrine (Frankfurter 1998: 134-5 on such shrines). Other examples in the form of houses or shrines have been found from Roman Egypt.

Compare: Bailey 1988: Q2001, 245 pl. 41.

69 Steatite bowl with image of Harpocrates (top)

Width 7.6 cm
First century AD
Provenance known, Egypt
Given by the Friends of the Fitzwilliam Museum
E.1.1981

The bowl is carved on the exterior with a central rosette and tongues radiating from a defining band possibly intended to represent a rosette.

The interior is decorated with a half figure of the god Harpocrates, carved in relief and placed slightly off-centre. Surrounding this is a similar pattern of a wreath and tongue designs radiating to the edges of the bowl. There is a second wreath around the rim and two ornate handles in the form of volutes. On the lower section of the rim is a small spout to guide liquid from the central tondo.

Harpocrates wears a skirt around his waist and holds the club of Hercules or a cornucopia in his left hand. His right hand is raised to his mouth and his index finger touches his lips. He also wears the double Crown of Upper and Lower Egypt. He appears to emerge from the centre of the vessel, possibly indicating his birth from a lotus flower, which is found on lamps of this period (Bailey 1988: Q2051, 250 pl. 43).

70 Steatite bowl with images of a Ram and Zeus Ammon (bottom)

Width 6.1 cm
First century AD
Provenance unknown, Egypt
E.S.110

The outside of the vessel is decorated with a carved rosette on the base. The outer walls are missing.

The inner face of the bowl is decorated with two figures, carved in relief. On the viewer's left is a representation of a bearded male with ram's horns, who can be identified as Zeus Ammon. On the right is a ram-headed deity. Both gods wear a Roman toga and *fibula* (brooch), thus illustrating the adoption and Romanisation of Egyptian gods by the Roman cultural repertoire.

These steatite bowls make their first appearance in the early Roman period. Many examples have a small spout on the lower rim that suggests liquid might have passed over the image of the god and flowed away via the spout. In this way, it seems that the bowls might have had a ritual function. There are other examples of water being used to bring the powers of a god into effect.

Compare: Rausch ed. 1998: 160 no. 100. Further reading: Parlasca 1983: 151-60.

The inundation of the Nile

71 Faience 'New Year' Flask

Height 6.7 cm
570-526 BC
Provenance unknown, Egypt
Given by R.G. Gayer-Anderson
E.GA.3093.1943

This small mould-made faience flask is decorated with the cartouche and name of the sixth ruler of the Twenty-sixth Dynasty, Ahmose Khnemibre, who is perhaps better known by his Greek name Amasis.

These flasks were offered on the first day of the Egyptian New Year, when they were filled with sacred water. The New Year was marked by the first full moon following the reappearance of the Dog Star (Greek Sirius or Egyptian Sothis) above the horizon. The New Year was connected to the annual inundation of the river Nile. The date of the flood varied from year to year, but would typically start in late June and last until October. It was essential for the prosperity of crops and was thus an important event in the Egyptian calendar. The Egyptians believed that the flooding represented the tears of the goddess Isis, mourning the murder of Osiris by their brother Seth.

During the annual flood the king of Egypt was not permitted to travel on the Nile. This tradition was still relevant in the Roman period and so when the Emperor Hadrian arrived in Egypt in AD 130 he waited until the flood had receded before setting out on his journey up river.

Compare: Bianchi in Friedman ed. 1998: 229-30 and 138 no. 126-127.

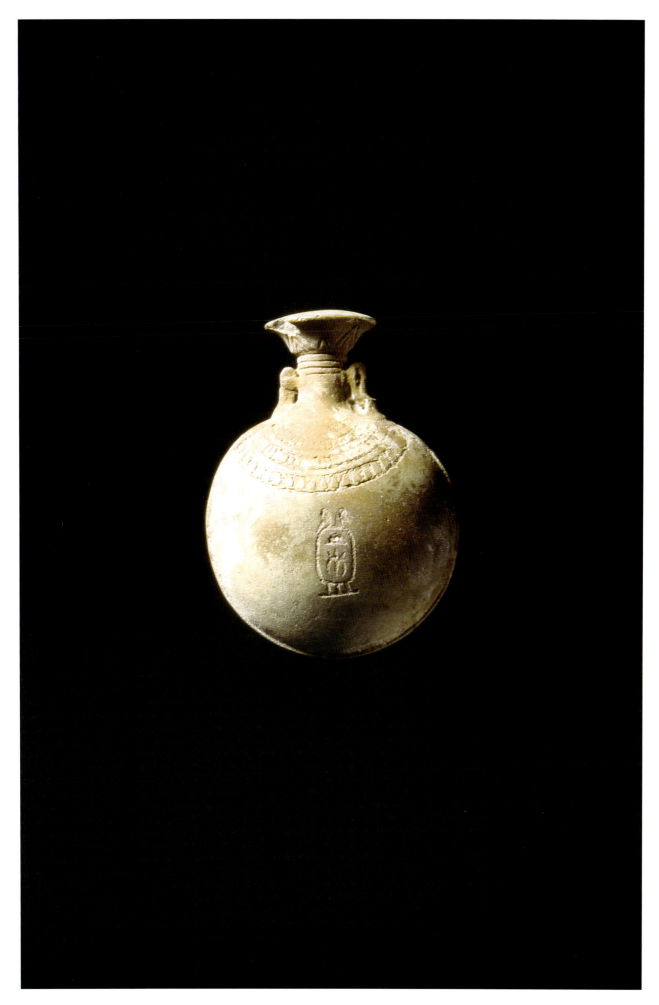

72 Clay oil lamp decorated with a frog and corn motif

Length 7.0 cm
First to third century AD*
Baboon galleries, North Saqqara
Given by the Egypt Exploration Fund
E.18.1971

Mould-made in two halves from Nile silt clay; there are burn marks around the nozzle. There is a maker's mark in the form of an alpha on the base.

The shoulders of the lamp are decorated with the rear end of a frog, with two legs clearly protruding from its prominent lower torso. Instead of front legs and a head, there are ears of corn. The frog may well have been associated with the inundation of the Nile and corn is often used to represent fertility and also wealth. It seems likely therefore that the combined symbolism celebrated the annual flood and its resulting prosperity.

Compare Petrie 1905: pl. LXIV no. 2-46; Bailey 1988: Q2103-2116, 257 pl. 46-47.

73 Clay oil lamp decorated with a frog

Length 8.1 cm
First to third century AD
Naukratis
Given by the Egypt Exploration Fund
GR.200.1899

Mould-made in two halves from Nile silt clay. There are considerable traces of a plaster wash on the surface with some black pigment on the head of the frog and on the legs. It is possible that the spots representing the frog's skin were all filled with black pigment, contrasting with the white of the plaster wash. There is a schematic inscribed maker's mark on the base.

The form of the frog is more naturalistic than many of the combined frog and corn lamps. The skin is finished with a dappled effect to indicate texture.

Frog, and related, lamps are traditionally dated to the third century AD, according to excavations at Karanis. It is, however, possible that these lamps were produced earlier in the Roman period (Ashton 2003: 4-5).

Compare Petrie 1905: pl. LXIII no. 77; Bailey 1988: Q2136, 259 pl. 48.

74 Clay oil lamp decorated with a boss and palm motif

Length 8.1
First to third centuries AD*
Naukratis
Given by the Egypt Exploration Fund
GR.211.1899

Mould-made from a buff-coloured marl clay. The base has delaminated. The shoulders are decorated with a motif that has been identified as two inter-twined palm leaves. In form it is similar to the frog and corn and frog lamps (cat. 72-73).

Part of the wick is preserved in the nozzle and what appears to have been the air hole clay, which would have been pushed through to form a hole at the centre of the lamp.

Compare: Petrie 1905: pl. LXV no. 2-27; Bailey 1988: Q2187-2192, 264 pl. 50-51.

75 Faience plate

Diameter 17 cm
First century AD
Provenance unknown
Given by R.G. Gayer-Anderson
E.GA.3097.1943

Part of the rim and inlays from the tondo are missing.

This mould-made faience plate is typical of the form that appears from the early first century AD. It is whiter and grittier than earlier forms of faience, or what are more correctly termed glazed wares, and represents a change in the 'recipe' at some point soon after the Roman occupation of Egypt (see cat. 7).

The inside is decorated with a series of symbols that are in sunken relief, perhaps suggesting that they were originally inlaid. They now reveal the quartz core of the material.

There are two pots filled with a palm branch, perhaps representing a tree. Between them is a krater, on which stands a duck or goose. If the latter then this may be a reference to the god Geb, whose name includes this symbol and who appears in human form with the crown of a goose on his head. Geb was a creator god and so would complement the other features on the plate. Above the bird is a fish (compare cat. 62), and to the lower left of the scene there appears to be a snake, perhaps a cobra. All of these symbols represent fertility and can be associated with the annual flooding of the Nile. It is possible that this plate served a ritual purpose either as part of a cult activity or as a votive to celebrate or ensure the inundation.

Faience was often used for cult vessels, although in the Roman period it becomes common in a limited variety of forms of plain vessels (Ashton 2003: 53-55). Faience is technically a glazed material with a non-ceramic core, and usually consists of a mixture of quartz pebbles, which are ground and then mixed with alkali or soda and lime to form a mouldable object that would then be glazed and fired. In the Roman period the glaze is usually applied by brush or dipping and is often uneven in application. On this particular vessel the core is visible around the inner rim and yet the glaze has accumulated on the underside, probably having dripped down during the manufacturing process and before it was fired.

Further reading: Ashton 2003: 53-56.

76 Terracotta figure of a dog (right)

Height 6.7 cm
Second to mid-fourth century AD
Hawara
Given by the British School of Archaeology in Egypt
E.98.1911

Nile silt clay, mould-made in three sections: front and two sides from the shoulders to back legs. The hollow feet have also been sealed with two slabs of clay. There is a small hole at the dog's rear, possibly to function as an air hole during firing.

There are traces of a plaster wash and red pigment on the surface. This small dog would have been completely painted. It has a curled tail and pointed ears. A collar and either amulet or bell is only just distinguishable but typical of this form of figurine. The legs are modelled in two pairs so that the figure stands easily. This feature suggests a fairly late date, and comparable examples were found at the city of Karanis in the Fayoum, in a level dating from AD 250-350. It is possible, however, that they were manufactured from an earlier date.

Dogs were associated with the star Sirius (Egyptian Sothis), whose rising was linked with the flooding of the Nile. Such images therefore have associations with fertility and also, through Isis, with the afterlife (Török 1995: 172-73). Terracotta figures of dogs are found as early as the Predynastic period (Desroches-Noblecourt 1999: 63) in Egypt, but they become especially prevalent in the Roman period, when they adopt a classical form and manufacturing technique.

Compare: Dunand 1990: 287-93 no. 861-80; Török 1995: 172-73 no. 279-81; Égypte Romaine 1997: 108-09 no. 109-10.
Further reading: Ashton 2003: 87.

77 Terracotta figure of a dog (left)

Height 7.1 cm
Second to mid-fourth century AD
Provenance unknown
Given by R.G. Gayer-Anderson
E.GA.2932.1943

There is some surface loss and no traces of pigment or plaster. The figure is hollow with an unsealed base. Like the last this figurine is made from Nile silt clay, mould-made in two sections, which unusually divide down the middle of the dog rather than having a separate front and back. Its breed and form, however, are quite different. The tail is curled but the legs are less robust, probably because the dog stands on a square, hollow base. The collar is prominent and a small bell or amulet can be seen. This dog has a much narrower neck and a smaller head than the last. It has been suggested that some of these images represent specific breads of dog. This long-haired variety might represent the Maltese spitz.

Further reading: Fjeldhagen (1995) 184-85, no. 183-85.

119

78 Copper alloy figurine of a dog

Height 5.6 cm
Second to fourth centuries AD
Provenance unknown
Purchased from Sir William Matthew Flinders Petrie
E.I.1900

This solid cast copper alloy figure appears to have been attached to another object, from which it has broken off at the feet. It is possible that it once belonged to a vessel, a candelabrum, or an oil lamp. 'Sprues', as they are called, such as those on the ends of the dog's feet can also result from the manufacturing process where the metal fills channels in the mould.

The figure is clearly canine, but shows an interesting mix of two forms: a wolf and a dog, of the type associated with Sirius and produced in large numbers in terracotta form (cat. 76-77). The reference could also be to the Sabine wolf, which, according to legend, suckled Romulus and Remus the first kings of Rome.

Like the terracotta figurines this dog wears an amulet around its neck. The prominent teats however are closer to the Sabine wolf so common in Roman iconography. The long tufts of hair on the face of the dog and pointed ears accord with the more common type (76). Because the figure can be associated with an Egyptian context we must presume that the artist may have aimed to produce the regular form of dog but was influenced by the Roman iconography.

Foreigners and captives

79 Limestone attachment in the form of a bound Libyan captive

Height 11.2 cm
Dynasty 3? (2686-2613 BC)
Provenance unknown, Egypt
Purchased through the University Purchase Fund
E.5.1972

The arms are missing and there is some damage to the front of the legs. Parts of the surface are worn.

This small stone figure represents one of the traditional enemies of Egypt. The long hair resting on the shoulders identifies the subject as a Libyan, who has been captured and bound. The hands are tied behind the back and the subject kneels. The feet are twisted in a manner that suggests the ankles are broken.

At the top of the head is a small tenon, which suggests that the figure formed part of a larger object, perhaps a chair. Such images regularly appear on statues, furniture and thresholds of buildings. Similar images can also be found on temple reliefs.

The ancient Egyptians traditionally believed that there were four races: Nubians, Libyans, Asiatics and themselves. Collectively foreigners were believed to threaten the order of the Egyptian world. They often appear as bound captives on the base of thrones and funerary cases or even on tiles, where they would be literally trampled under-foot. Pharaohs are often shown smiting their foreign enemies whilst holding them by their hair.

Foreigners were, however, an important element of Egyptian society from Dynasty 6 (about 2300-2150 BC) onwards. At this period Libyans and Nubians joined the army as mercenaries. During Dynasty 26 (664-525 BC) Greeks were allowed to settle at Naukratis in the Delta; in this trading post they established Greek sanctuaries and worshipped Greek gods. In the sixth century BC Carians from southwest Asia Minor (Turkey) settled at Memphis and lived amongst Egyptians.

Several foreign dynasties ruled Egypt, namely Hyksos (1650-1550 BC), Libyans (1069-664 BC), Kushites from modern-day Sudan (747-656 BC), Persians (525-404 BC and 343-332 BC), and Macedonian Greeks (332-30 BC). Like the Persians the Romans were non-resident pharaohs, but for a much longer period of time. It is perhaps because of their interest in Egyptian culture that there is an increase in production of images involving foreigners.

Vassilika 1995: 18-19 no. 5.

80 Fired clay execration figure

Height 12 cm
Middle Kingdom-Second Intermediate Period (2055-1551 BC)
Provenance unknown
Given by G.D. Hornblower
E.189.1939

The right arm and left hand are broken and repaired.

Hand-modelled figure decorated with incised marks to indicate hair and punched marks representing tattoos. The subject wears an irregular wig the style of which finds close parallels in the wigs worn in painted or carved images of the Hyksos. During the Second Intermediate Period many of these people settled in the Egypt bringing with them their culture (see cat. 79). They are often depicted in art of the period wearing a short striated wig, which would be represented here in an abbreviated form. It has been suggested (Vassilika) that the subject of this figure is female on account of the prominent pubic triangle and tattoos. The lack of breasts is typical of the period. The eyes are pressed unevenly in the clay and a single cut and modelling of the area around the chin indicate the mouth. The nose is similarly pinched out of the clay.

A strip of clay binds the hands behind the back. The ankles are also pressed together but here the clay rope is missing. It is thought that such figures functioned as part of execration rituals and this idea would accord with the depiction of the bound foreign foe. Although the modelling of the piece is artistically crude, the attention to detail endows this small figure with considerable character.

Vassilika 1995: 44-45 no. 18.

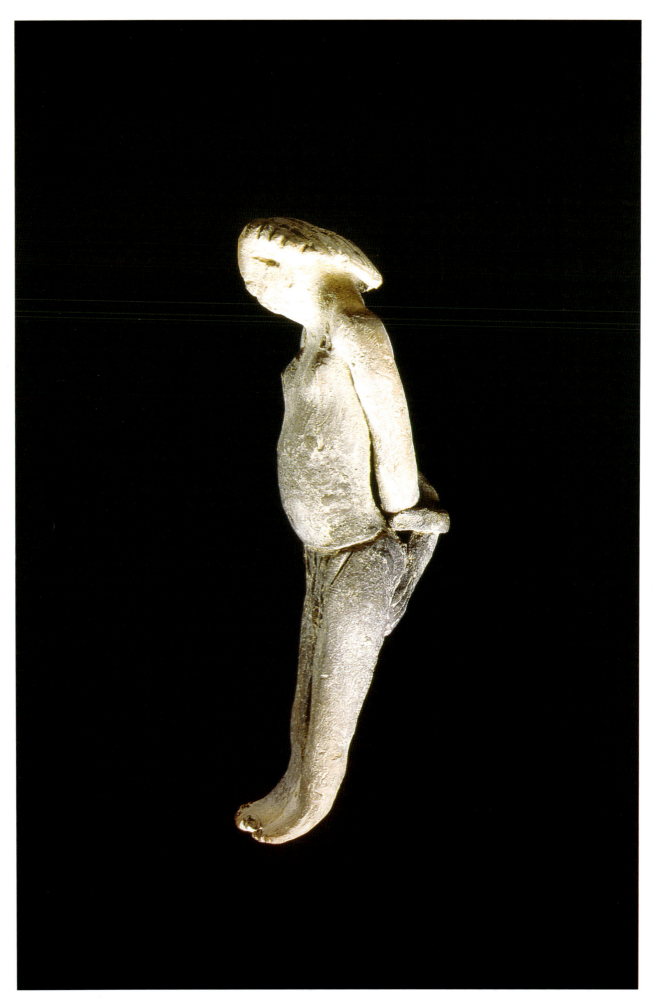

81 Cartonnage foot case showing two bound captives

Height 25 cm
First century AD
Hawara
Given by the British School of Archaeology in Egypt
E.103b.1911

There is some surface damage around the edges and on the upper section of the front panel. There are stains of a resinous material that appears to be ancient on the bottom and the sides.

The bottom of the foot-case is decorated with two bound and naked captives: a Libyan on the left and an Asiatic on the right. The two are tethered together by a chain. The Libyan is identified by his shoulder-length hair, curled at the end, and his long beard. He stands on his right foot, his left leg is raised and bound to the back of his right thigh and the arms are held together at his back and tied together at the top. The Asiatic can be identified by his short wig and pointed beard. He stands facing the Libyan but is bound in a different way: his wrists are tied behind his back and his right leg is raised and tied in front of him to his left thigh. Between the two captives is a rectangular panel decorated with a floral motif.

The front of the foot-case is divided into panels decorated with rosettes, lozenges and wadjet eyes with a central lotus flower and bud motif. At the top are two gold feet, a reference to the use of gold in the embalming process, and two bands perhaps representing the lower section of a garment. Some examples of foot-cases show the sandals but on this particular example the feet are bare. The feet are surrounded by cross-hatching, decorated in diagonal bands of black, pink, blue and white pigment.

The mummy to which the foot-case belongs was found by Sir William Matthew Flinders Petrie during his excavations at Hawara in the Faiyum. It was placed within a two-room tomb with five other bodies, a further two being placed one on top of the other in a smaller chamber. Petrie wrote in his publication of the finds: '[Grave] F was a unique burial with cartonnage head-piece unusually large, having a wreath of loose leaves of gilt canvas and green berries between them, in the hands a red wreath and a candle. The rhombic bandage was in five layers with gilt buttons, and two rows of buttons on the chest. The foot-case was gilt. (Cambridge).' The cartonnage torso and head is also preserved in the Fitzwilliam Museum. The whereabouts of the mummy with its 'rhombic' dressings is unknown and it may have been left on the site.

Images of bound captives standing in this manner were common from the New Kingdom onwards and can be compared with the earlier kneeling captives of the Old Kingdom (cat. 79). Although such imagery was originally reserved for kings, by the Roman period many private individuals were shown with foreign captives at their feet and in some instances the mummies are shown wearing the royal *uraeus*.

Petrie (1911b) 3-4, pl. XXIII, 6 F; Grimm 1974: 127.
Compare: Égypte Romaine 1997: 164-65 no. 189.

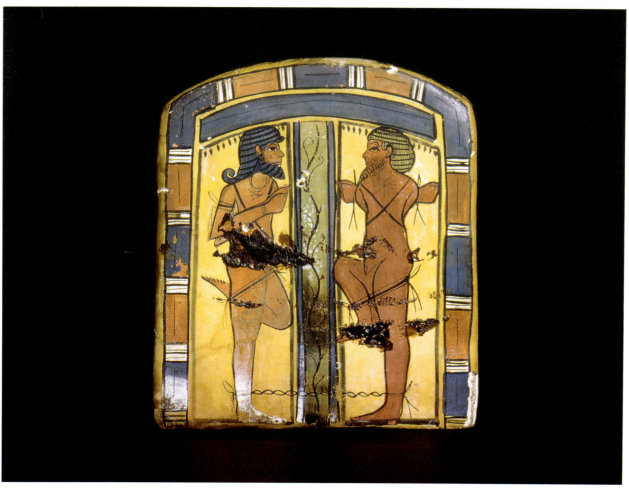

82 Fragment of a terracotta figure of a Nubian

Height 7.7 cm
Dated by the excavator to the fourth century AD, but more likely to be second to third century AD.
House 'F' Ehnasya
Given by the Egypt Exploration Fund
E.122.1904

Mould-made Nile silt clay terracotta figure of a Nubian, modelled on both sides and well-preserved but with no traces of plaster wash or pigment. Only the head and upper torso are preserved.

This small terracotta figurine shows a well-known type: that of a Nubian soldier or warrior, who holds a double-headed axe. In form and style the figurine sits more comfortably within the classical repertoire, even though the subject is common in Egypt. The find-spot and Nile silt clay also confirm that this was made in Egypt. It possibly served a decorative purpose in the house where it was found.

In his publication of the house where this figure was found Petrie notes that there were coins, fragments of blown and moulded glass and pottery dating to the fourth century AD, however, as with other terracotta figurines, this example can be dated on stylistic grounds to an earlier period.

Black Africans appear in both ancient Greek and Egyptian artistic traditions and can be distinguished by their thick curly hair and facial features, which consisted of a broad nose and prominent lips. This form became a genre for representing the Nubians, who came from modern-day Sudan. In paintings they are often shown with black or dark brown skin. In earlier periods of Egyptian art Nubian men and women are often represented as captives of Egypt, and as such appear on statue bases, thrones and temple reliefs.

Many ancient Egyptians would today be described as 'black', but Egyptian art and its rigid canons showed subjects of the king in a stylised manner, often reflecting the facial features found on his own statues. Thus we only really have these caricatures on which to base our knowledge of the presentation of this group of Egyptians. The exceptions to this are the Kushite rulers of the Twenty-fifth Dynasty. Some scholars have suggested that the facial features on portraits of this royal family are more African than those of other dynasties. A comparison may be made with earlier sculpture from the Middle Kingdom, where a similarly so-called veristic style was incorporated into the royal repertoire but is unlikely to have offered a realistic representation of the subject (see cat. 11). Strong evidence of archaising during the Twenty-fifth dynasty might go some way to explaining the re-appearance of this form of sculpture. However, it is unlikely that we will ever know for certain why artists showed the rulers in this way.

Petrie 1905: 27, pl. XLV no. 9
Compare: Petrie 1905: 27, pl. L no. 110-12 for three similar figures from house H, which was also dated to the fourth century AD; Dunand 1990: 222-24 no. 610, 614-17; Török 1995: 156-57, no. 239.

83 Terracotta mask of a boy wearing an eastern cap

Height 9 cm
First to second centuries AD
Possibly from Denderah
Given by the Wellcome Trustees
E. 432.1982

Mould-made terracotta fragment of a male head, broken at the neck and without a back. The chin and nose are damaged. Inside, finger prints and ridges show how the clay was pushed into the mould. There are traces of white plaster wash and red pigment on the face and headdress. The hat is damaged at the front.

The face is a caricature of a youthful male subject. The cheeks are prominent and fleshy, and the brow is high with prominent lines. The lips are forced into a smile that reveals a hint of a dimple on the chin. The eyes are large and the pupils are defined, a feature common in Egyptian stone sculpture prior to the Roman period, but found more commonly in Roman art from the second century AD. (Bianchi in Bianchi ed. 1988: 131 no. 36)

The only identifiable feature is the hat, which is of a pointed variety often associated with Phrygians or Greek peoples from the East. It seems therefore likely that this head was a caricature of an eastern race. The hair is short and indicated by a series of wavy lines on the areas left uncovered by the hat.

The head does not appear ever to have had a back. It is likely that it served a decorative function at the centre of a roundel or architectural medallion. It is larger than most terracotta figures but it shares a common theme with many other images of racial types that were produced during the Greek and Roman occupations of Egypt. Many, like this example, reveal a comical aspect as indicated by the exaggerated facial features. Török (1995: 34 no. 34) publishes a similar head, which is described as a representation of one of the Dioskuroi (the twin sons of Zeus from Greek mythology) from a votive clay shield. Masks of actors also exist (Dunand 1990: 219-21 no. 601-07).

130

84 Clay amphora

Height 45 cm
Second-Fourth century AD?
Provenance unknown
Given by A.G.W. Murray
E.155.1913

Part of the rim is missing. The order of descriptions around the vessel is from the viewer's perspective.

The decoration on this wheel-made amphora is something of a mystery. The entire surface is covered in a variety of unusual figures and phrases moulded in low relief. The vessel is published here for the first time with photographs and drawings, partly in the hope that parallels might be found for it.

The vessel was brought to Cambridge in 1913 by a member of Trinity College: A.G.W. Murray. A note accompanying the vessel describes it as 'an ancient Egyptian amphora of large size and rough workmanship used for carrying water from the Nile by the women of the country'.

The script contains predominantly Greek characters but there are additional non-Greek letter forms, possibly imitating hieroglyphs. The inscriptions might be thought likely to offer a clue as to the identity of the characters, but on the occasions when the iconography is intelligible the inscriptions do not seem to correspond.

It is likely that this vessel functioned as a ritual or magical amphora and that each figure meant something to the original owner or user. Many of the figures have parallels in Egyptianising statuary and wall paintings from Italy, especially dating to the late first and second centuries AD. There are parallels in stone for this type of object, such as a large basalt krater, excavated at Hadrian's Villa near Rome and now housed in the Capitoline Museums, Rome.

Side A:

fig. a

[fig. a] Central scene, upper register: a giant seated figure of the Roman god Pan, who was half-man half-goat and who features commonly in bucolic scenes, often playing pipes (cat. 31). Here, Pan brandishes a club. To the viewer's right is a front-facing female figure wearing a lotus crown and shoulder-length wig, she holds a smaller club in her left hand and rests her right on the seat occupied by Pan. Her mouth is open indicating aggression and in some respects she mimics the god Bes (cat. 59). To the left of Pan is an elderly male figure seen in three-quarter view towards Pan. He holds either a knife or a smaller version of the club. He wears a loosely fitting garment exposing a flabby upper torso. His hair is unkempt and rests on his shoulders and he appears to have a whiskery beard. Beneath this group is an inscription, punctuated by depictions of swallows, all facing left.

[fig. b] A large-scale figure of Harpocrates turns away from the main scene towards the handle. He can be identified by the finger-to-mouth pose and also by the traditional *ḥm.ḥm.t* crown that he wears (see cat. 44-46). He also wears an abbreviated form of the *nemes* headcloth and appears to hold something in his left hand. Apart from his headdress he is naked. His position suggests he is seated. Beneath him is a line of text in Greek letters.

fig. b

[fig. c] Central scene, lower register: a bald and naked male figure stands facing the viewer. In his left

fig. c

fig. d

arm he holds a small deer and a crane by their necks; the bird's feet are placed on the ground. The man's right arm is raised and his fist appears to be clenched. It is possible that he represents a priest on account of the lack of clothes and hair. To the right of the central figure is a mummiform figure wearing a sun disk and possibly cow's horns; this area of the surface is very worn. To the left of the central figure is a second figure wearing long robes, a *nemes* headcloth and the Crowns of Upper and Lower Egypt. It is possible that he represents Harpocrates.

[fig. d] Central scene, neck: there is a central panel decorated with a text and birds, facing left. There are two further birds on top of the panel, standing and with lowered heads. Beneath the text is a leaping goat, and to the left a bull's head perhaps representing signs of the zodiac. There is also a text around the lip of the vessel;

[fig. e] Moving right from side A, the handle forms a focal point. Beneath it is a winged bird with a human head wearing a headdress of either horns or two cobras flanking an ovoid shape. This bird is known in Egyptian theology as the Ba bird. The Egyptians believed that the Ba was one of the elements of the human soul and that after death it left the body in which it was later reunited in the after life. Figures of Ba birds were thus common in funerary iconography. A single letter is readable beneath the figure.

fig. e

[fig. f] To the left of the handle a standing figure faces the viewer, but turns away from the main central scene. S/he wears a *nemes* headcloth with striated lappets reminiscent of those found on statuary in Rome during the second century AD and was worn by both male and female subjects during this period. The figure wears a long, belted garment, with no indication of sleeves, perhaps indicating that only the lower part of the body is covered. The right hand rests on the belt and the left arm is bent at the elbow with the hand gesturing

upwards, perhaps towards the central figure of Pan. Like Pan, this figure is shown in the larger scale. Below the figure is part of the text reading UC...C (the C probably a lunate sigma). This figure is shown on the same large scale as Pan.

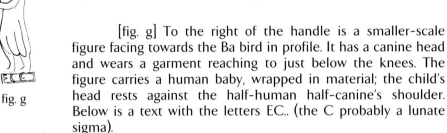

[fig. g] To the right of the handle is a smaller-scale figure facing towards the Ba bird in profile. It has a canine head and wears a garment reaching to just below the knees. The figure carries a human baby, wrapped in material; the child's head rests against the half-human half-canine's shoulder. Below is a text with the letters EC.. (the C probably a lunate sigma).

fig. g

fig. f

[fig. h right] The handle is decorated at the top with a frontal facing animal head. The animal has large pointed ears and sticks its tongue out. Below this head is a mummiform figure wearing a nemes headdress and holding a sceptre in its left hand. The subject has a beak-like nose. Standing in front of this figure is a second wearing a *modius* on its head and a garment with cross-hatching on the skirt. The arms are positioned to the side and slightly in front of the body in a relaxed pose. This type of positioning usually indicates that the larger figure is protecting the smaller. A text is positioned below.

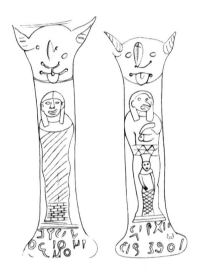

fig. h

Side B:

[fig. i] Central scene, upper register: the central figure stands behind a pillar, decorated with four panels. From the bottom: a bird, a frontal human head with mouth open in aggression, two unidentifiable animal (?) figures. The pillar is supported at either side by a dog standing on its hind legs. The figure appears to hold two clubs and wears a headdress, now difficult to see. The feet peep out from below the pillar and below this is an inscription in Greek lettering.

fig. i

[fig. j] The composition of this side differs from that of side A the figures on either side of the central scene face inwards, implying that they are part of it. To the left is a pair of naked figures, one clearly male. They are accompanied by a small pyramidal shaped object, possibly a cake (?) and a bird (possibly a goose or duck) which looks up towards them. The male figure wears a pointed hat and beard; his facial features are almost mask-like in appearance. In his left hand he holds what appears to be a knife; this is positioned above the head of the bird. The second human figure holds onto the first by his wrist. He is naked but without genitals or breasts. It can be assumed that he is male because of his shaven head. Below this scene is an inscription in Greek lettering.

fig. k

fig. j

[fig. k] So far all the figures on side B have been small in scale. To the left of the main scene, however, is a larger-scale male figure. He wears an animal head as a headdress (possibly a dog or wolf) and a cloak also made from animal skin. He stands with his weight on his left leg with the right leg relaxed. The left arm is bent at the elbow and the hand up-turned. The right arm is extended outwards and holds a small round object, possibly a fruit offering. There is text below. In front of this figure is a small scale image of a cow's head, possibly a reference to the zodiac.

[fig. l] Central panel, lower register: five figures occupy the lower register on side B. From the left is a group of three, accompanied by a bird which

stands mid-air close to the shoulder of the figure on the far left. This figure has a bull's head and wears a crown of horns, sun disk and plumes. The body is anthropoid; the figure's legs turn to the right and are placed together. The upper torso is turned towards the viewer giving the impression that the figure is twisting.

fig. l

The left hand is held loosely across the abdomen and the right arm is held at the side, away from the body. In style this figure is similar to a granite statue of Apis now held in the Vatican Museums and dating to the second century AD. Unusually the statue, like this figure, shows a bovine head on a human body.

[fig. l] On the same level as this figure is a second who turns towards the opposite direction. He is naked except for the crown of Upper Egypt. He stands in an awkward position with the right foot crossed over the left and the left arm drawn towards his crotch. His right arm is bent at the elbow and he holds a baton or stick, which rests against his shoulder. He is bearded with a prominent moustache and is elderly in appearance.

fig. m

[fig l] Between these two figures is a mummiform figure, possibly representing a coffin. The figure wears the usual *nemes* headcloth and the lower section of the body is decorated with a brick-like pattern, perhaps imitating mummy wrappings. Under this figure is the Greek letter omega; the rest of the text is missing.

[fig. l] The remaining two figures, moving right, are also both mummiform. The first, who occupies a central position on the lower register, wears a striated *nemes* headcloth and a funerary beard. His arms are crossed across his chest and he holds two sticks, presumably a crook and flail. There is a text beneath him. [fig. m] The figure to the extreme right is larger than the rest of the group. In addition to the usual headdress and a funerary beard he also wears an elaborate headdress consisting of a lunar disk with two (?) birds joined from a single body. Their plumes are connected and decorated with two further disks.

[fig. m] Next to this final figure is a tall object with a bulbous base, perhaps a reference to a Nilometer, an instrument which measured the extent of the river Nile. Nilometers were typically carved onto stone walls but also appear on Roman mosaics in a number of forms.

Central panel, neck: [fig. n] The neck is decorated with a large-scale winged figure who has an animal head and wears a partially striated *nemes* headcloth. The head is difficult to identify but the figure also has pendulous breasts, similar to those of the hippopotamus headed goddess Taweret or the male Nile god Hapi. The hands are positioned in front and point towards a second smaller figure. This figure has a bald head and is possibly mummiform. There is a text beneath the two with recognisable Greek letters.

fig. n

To the right of the central registers is the second handle (fig. h left). This is decorated with a single mummiform figure with a cross hatched coffin or wrappings and a brick-pattern base. The figure wears a plain nemes headdress and the face is shown with an archaising smile; there is a text below. Above the figure is an animal head with its tongue sticking out.

[fig. q] To the left of the main scene is a figure whose body faces the viewer but who turns his head to the left. It wears a long garment and has the head possibly of Anubis. Two snakes rear towards the subject, one on each side and there is a line of unintelligible text beneath. It is possible, if the head is a mask, that this figure represents a priest dressing as the god Anubis. Wall paintings and statues from Italy show similar figures and offer a parallel for this individual (Alfano in Walker and Higgs 2000: 243 no.IV.15 and 245-47 no.IV.20).

fig. q

[fig. o] Below the handle is a dancing satyr with long beard and bald head. He stands with his left leg forward, steadied by the ball of his right foot. His left arm is held out and his hand holds what appears to be a flail or branch. The right arm is raised and the hand holds a vessel, from which a liquid is poured into the mouth of a crane. Satyrs were

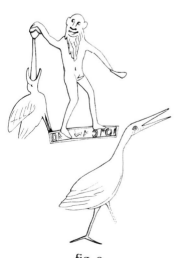

fig. o

woodland creatures who were associated with the rites of Dionysos and are often shown in processions, his action here may be a reference to such an event.

Behind the handles are two further figures: [fig. p] the first handle region is decorated with two associated figures. Both have beaks but appear to be human and mummiform. The larger figure on the viewer's left turns towards the smaller and holds an object in his left hand towards his chest. The smaller figure wears a triangular hat and has a brick-like design on his body. It is possible that the heads are also intended to represent masks, perhaps of the god Thoth, who was often shown with an ibis head. Here, however the larger bird appears closer to a crane.

fig. r

[fig. r] Behind the second handle that is decorated with a single mummiform figure, is a male with sagging breasts and flabby upper torso. He wears a headdress of antlers and in his hands he holds a long knife or club. His lower section appears to be mummiform and is inscribed with a text, now too worn to read.

fig. p

Compare el-Daly in Ucko and Champion eds. 2003: 48 fig. 3:2 for a fourteenth-century interpretation of a Middle Kingdom stela.

138

Personal piety

85 Fragment of a steatite statuette of a priest or official

Height 4 cm
First century BC-AD
Provenance unknown, Egypt
Given by the Friends of the Fitzwilliam Museum
E.46.1971

Only the head survives. The right eye, nose and mouth are damaged and there are signs of wear on the back pillar. There are also extensive light scratches on the surface with a substantial gouge below the jar line on the right side.

The neck and head are supported by a back pillar, indicating that its form is Egyptian in style. Representations of the king, his family and his officials are a standard Egyptian type of statue. In the Roman Imperial period, statues of emperors and private individuals often adopt features such as drapery, so-called 'portrait' features and hair that are not obviously Egyptian. Such features have a long history in Egyptian sculpture as shown by the Middle Kingdom statues of the Twelfth dynasty rulers, who appeared with the so-called veristic portrait type (see cat. 11).

The receding hairline is especially typical of representations of officials at the end of the Ptolemaic and start of the Roman period (30 BC). It is thought that Roman Republican portrait types may well have influenced this hairstyle, but it was also known in Egypt through the portraits of Ptolemy VIII. Here the hair is indicated not by carved curls, but rather by scratches on the surface. The square jaw, high cheekbones and sullen appearance of the mouth are all also typical of representations of the late first century BC.

It is likely that this small statue was placed in a temple or sanctuary and that its owner was an Egyptian who played an official role within society. Priests were traditionally shown with shaven heads, because they were expected to remove all body hair before tending to the gods. By the Roman period, however, they were often depicted with some hair.

Certain features suggest that an Egyptian artist carved this piece: namely the prominent eye-lines and almond-shaped sockets, the fleshy nose and holes at the corner of the mouth. All these elements are found in the Egyptian repertoire from the fourth century BC onwards: their continuation into the Roman period suggests that workshops sustained the Egyptian tradition.

Compare: Bothmer 1960: 170-72 no. 131 figs. 327-28; Etienne in Walker and Higgs eds. 2001: 178-79 no. 187 and Ashton and Andrews in Walker and Higgs eds. 2001: 182-83 no. 190.

Further reading: Bianchi in Bianchi ed. 1988: 55-80.

86 Terracotta figurine of a rider with palm

Height 15.1 cm
Dated by the excavator to circa 250 AD
'House K' Ehnasya.
Given by the Egypt Exploration Fund
E.124.1904

There are traces of plaster on the surface with a pinky red pigment on the palm branch, the head and the back of the left leg.

Nile silt clay, mould-made figure manufactured in two halves and joined together. The right arm is missing and there is some damage to the back of the palm branch. A small hole between the legs may either have been an air hole, or have facilitated the figure's attachment to a base or more likely an animal. The clay at the top of the right arm is roughened and the surface remains intact, suggesting that no arm was added. The surface continues down the side of the figure.

The male subject appears to have been sitting on the back of an animal. He wears a helmet or headdress and in his left arm he carries a palm branch. His costume is different from those usually worn by Egyptians, suggesting he represents a specific person or social group. Petrie, in the original publication of the piece, identified this figure as a representation of an acrobat (1905: 26).

This form of costume, consisting of trousers and tunic, with heavy folds is most commonly associated with Persians in Greek and Roman art. Egyptian artists depict this particular group with pointed hats. A series of terracotta figurines possibly dating to the second Persian period and from Memphis show the subjects on horse-back and with shields (Ashton 2003: 72). This figure from House K is clearly later but perhaps influenced by these earlier models.

The palm branch on this figurine suggests that the subject may be taking part in a festival of some kind. As we have already seen, this attribute was associated with the inundation of the Nile and appeared on both lamps and vessels during the Roman period (see cat. 74 and 75). It is also possible that his 'exotic' dress is a reference to the cult of Mithras and that he is an initiate of this religious sect (Harris 1996: 169-76). This figure's possible reference to culture outside Egypt is indicative of the multi-cultural society at this time and also of Egyptian artists' ability to produce subjects that were not exclusively linked to their own tradition.

Petrie 1905: 26 pl. LI no. 127.
Compare Dunand 1990: 221 no. 608 (horseman/coachman?).

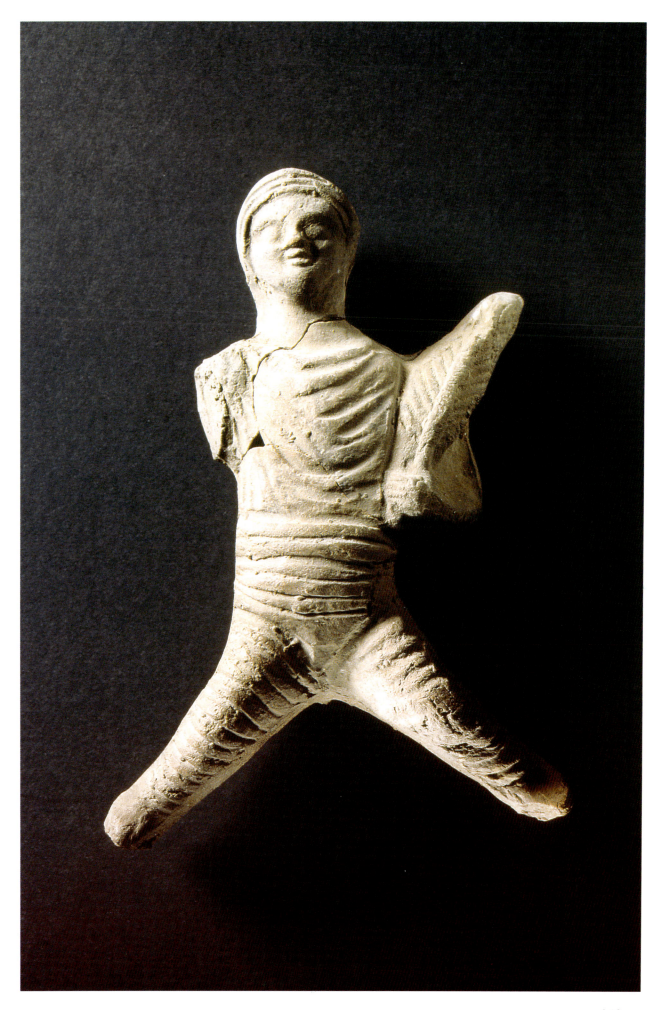

87 Painted wooden door panel

Height 26.3 cm
Date Second to third century AD?
Provenance unknown, Egypt
Given by R.G. Gayer-Anderson
E.GA.4332.1943

There are areas where the plaster and pigment are missing revealing the wooden door, this is especially prominent at the top where a modern stain has been applied to cover the patchy areas. The inside of the door is unpainted. An additional piece of wood at the top of the main section is fastened to the door with wooden dowels.

This small door was doubtless part of a *naos* (shrine) as indicated by the hole for a handle. It is likely that it was one of a pair of doors that protected a statue of a god. The exterior wood is covered with a plaster wash, forming a base for the painted decoration. The background is pink, over which two sets of vertical stripes in yellow and red, perhaps intended to represent a door. In the middle stands a male figure. He is unlikely to be a priest because he has a full head of thick curly black hair. The hair is indicated by painted black curls on top of a layer of grey wash. His robes are not of the formal or official kind, so that it seems likely that he is intended to represent a private individual or worshipper. His green tunic is short-sleeved and is pulled up to his knees by a yellow belt, shown as a ribbon tied around his hips. The tunic is finished with black tassels around the hem, sleeves and around the neck. The belt is yellow, shown as a ribbon tied around his hips. His hands are raised, he holds cymbals, and he is clearly intended to be part of a religious parade. He stands on the balls of his feet, a sign that he is to be thought of as dancing. The eye is shown frontally even though the body is in profile. The skin is given a lustrous appearance by what appears to be the mineral orpiment scattered on the surface. This layer has been placed over the black outlines and was perhaps added as part of the finishing touches for the piece.

Like Egyptian-style paintings the subject here is shown in profile view. However, the tunic, and style of painting are much closer to Roman depictions. There is a freedom of movement often missing from Egyptian art. Such images would have been common in both the Ptolemaic and Roman cities where many festivals took place around Egyptian temples and Greek sanctuaries. Accounts suggest that much wine flowed at such events, which were often inclusive of all members of the population. In form the *naos* to which this door belonged is Egyptian, but the style of painting is clearly within the Roman repertoire, showing a common joining of traditions during this time.

Further reading and comparison with tomb paintings: Venit 2002.

88 Limestone funerary stela

Height 29.5 cm
Third to fourth centuries AD
Said to be from Therenuthis (Kom Abu Billo)
Purchased through the Greg Fund
E.83.1975

There is superficial damage to the surface of the stone at the lower section of the front and back. The top of the front is roughly carved and the back surface is roughly finished. There are remains of a white plaster wash on the surface of the front of the stela and red pigment on the pine-cone, the offering table, the soles of the feet and the Anubis figure. On the garland are traces of pink pigment. Guide lines are visible below the columns and the figures stand out in relief from the background. An inscription would be expected in the lower register of the stela, but none was added.

This limestone funerary stela shows a seated female figure in an Egyptianising setting. She faces the viewer in a manner more typical of classical relief sculpture: the body is in a fully frontal pose. In Egyptian reliefs the subject is typically placed with the legs in profile and the upper torso twisted in three-quarter view. The subject on the Fitzwilliam Museum's relief also wears a Roman mantle and dress rather than a traditional Egyptian costume. In her left hand is a wreath suggesting that this is a funerary context and in her right hand she holds a pinecone or item of fruit on a simple conical offering table. Her left elbow appears to rest on the side of the chair. Her hair is shown in rows of curls that are typical of this period; on top of the head is a garland that falls onto the shoulders. It is likely that the seated figure is the deceased, making an offering to Anubis. This is also atypical of Egyptian stelae, where the deceased typically receives offerings from members of his or her family.

Confirming the funerary nature of this piece is the small jackal in the upper left corner. This represents the god Anubis, who elsewhere is often shown with an anthropoid body leading the deceased to the afterlife. This sketchy cartoon-like figure may represent a statue or the presence of the god himself. The building in which the deceased sits is reminiscent of the temples shown on Roman coinage (cat. 20-25). Here it may well be intended to indicate a tomb. The two columns are Egyptian lotus columns; these are surmounted by a rounded architrave, also found on the coin images of Egyptian-style temples. Tombs such as this were high status burials and it is possible that the owner of this small stela was not buried in such an ostentatious manner but that the artists intended to evoke the idea of a tomb entrance. The merging of Roman-style dress and pose with an Egyptianising building and god are typical of stelae during this period. Elements from both traditions were also often found in tomb design of non-Egyptian burials in cities such as Alexandria.

Martin forthcoming

Further reading: Schmidt 2003

89 Terracotta figure of a female offerant

Height 16.7 cm
First to second centuries AD
Said to have come from the Faiyum, Egypt
Purchased through the Greg Fund.
E.1.1995

Nile silt clay, mould-made and hand modelled. The surface is covered with a plaster wash and there are remains of red paint on the hem of the dress with further additions on the hair, bracelets and necklaces. There are traces of pink pigment in the folds of the cushion and on top of the cake on the offering table. The plaster wash is poorly preserved on the back and no traces of pigment remain. The back is, however, decorated with incised lines forming a pattern. There is an air hole to the proper right hand side at the back. There are drips of plaster on the inside of the figure.

The woman sits with her ankles together, knees splayed, and her hands raised in prayer. Usually figures in this position are naked and with an emphasis on the pubic triangle that connects the subject with fertility or presenting her as a concubine of the dead. This example is fully clothed and thus probably represents the deceased (Vassilika 1998: 124). The subject wears a short-sleeved full-length dress, and garlands on her head and around her neck. She wears ankle bands, armbands, bracelets, necklaces and earrings. The hair is divided by a central parting and pulled back into a bun, in a style typical of the early Roman period.

In front of the chair is a small offering table, containing loaves of bread and cakes. This idea was very much within the Egyptian tradition, but here the offerant and the style of the figure is heavily dependent upon Roman ideals. This type of object indicates a continuing but adapting tradition and is clear evidence for both the Romanisation of Egypt and also the acceptance of Egyptian ideas amongst Romans.

Vassilika 1998: 124-25 no. 60.
Compare Dunand 1990: 261, no. 276 (dated second century AD).

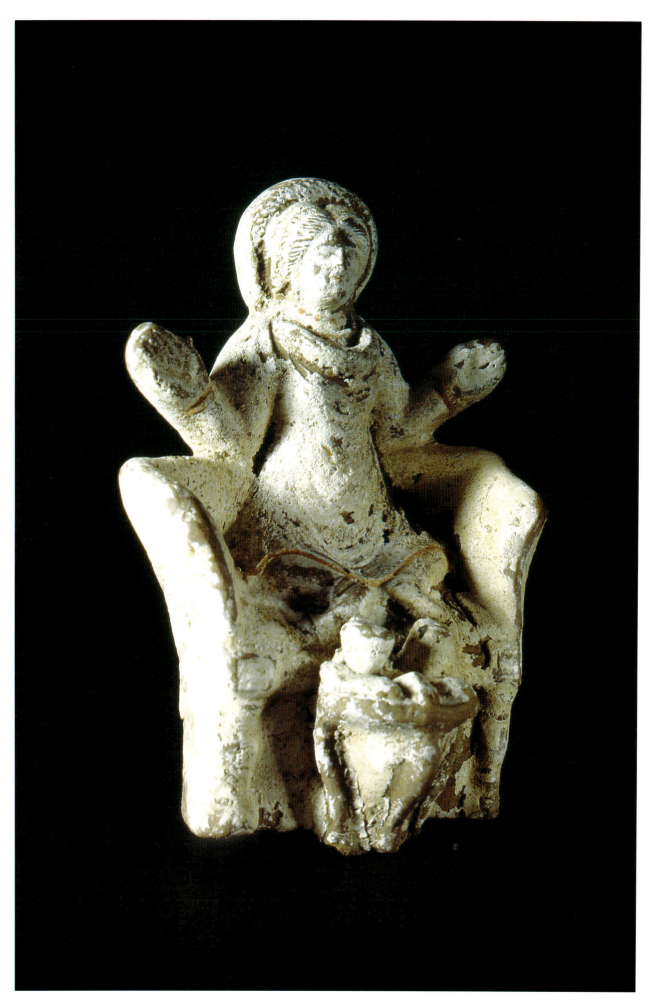

90 Terracotta figure of a female offerant

Height 13.1 cm
Third Century AD
Provenance unknown, Egypt
E.P.315

Nile silt clay, mould-made in two halves and then joined. The back is not modelled. Part of the back of the head is missing and the front edge of the base is broken. There are white accretions on the front and the lower back left hand side is spalled.

The figure is female and in some respects highly stylised in form. Her stumpy arms are raised in prayer and at first glance her lower abdomen seems to be directly attached to her feet. She is, however, seated and her ankles are placed together with her knees apart.

The figure wears a diaphanous dress, which appears to be short-sleeved. Her breasts are rounded and positioned close together at the centre of her chest, and her rounded abdomen is also visible. In addition to her dress the subject also wears jewellery: a necklace with three circular pendants, matching earrings and bracelets on both wrists. The hair is styled in a manner that is typical of the Severan period, hence the dating of the piece. It is not possible to tell whether the additional clay above the head is left over from the manufacturing process or intended to represent the festival garland, worn by many figures of this type.

Such figures are known as orantes figures (singular orans), from the Latin verb 'to pray': hence the raised arms. They appear in a variety of forms, some naked, others holding offerings. The stylised form of this particular example is typical of the later periods of Roman occupation.

In terms of their meaning their gesture suggests piety, and many also have a strong reference to fertility. This is suggested here by the prominent breasts and swollen abdomen. Other less subtle examples show the figures naked with legs apart. Most orantes figures are female although male examples have also been found.

Like many terracotta figures the orantes could either have functioned as votives or have been used within houses at domestic shrines. It is also possible that they were seen as charms of some kind. Some have been found in tombs where they functioned as grave goods. When Petrie discovered such figures during his excavations at Ehnasya (1905: 2) he wrote: 'no meaning has yet been given for these female figures, whether with hands raised or put down [pl. L.]107 is a doll...one was found in a child's grave with other toys at Hawara the others therefore may all be for toys'.

Further reading and compare: Török 1995: 127-30.

91 Terracotta female figure

Height 26.5 cm
New Kingdom (1550-1070 BC)
Provenance unknown
E.GA.278.1949
Bequeathed by R.G. Gayer-Anderson

Fine Nile slit clay. The figure was manufactured in two halves and then joined; the weight suggests that the body is hollow. The right arm is cracked and the left ear is missing. A triangular clay section representing hair is also missing. There are scratch marks on the surface of the back of the figure.

The feet are joined and a single incised line delineates the swollen thighs at the front and back. The arms are rolled out of clay; the left is positioned on the hip and the right rests on the abdomen, which is swollen. The breasts are modelled separately and attached high on the chest, close together. The eyes and mouth are represented by cuts in the clay with additional black and red pigment respectively. The nose and right ear were modelled separately. The eyebrows are pinched out of the clay. The forehead is high and the top of the skull is swollen in appearance, the socket at the top of the head would have originally held hair, perhaps that of the dead person in whose tomb this may have been placed. Tattoos are indicated by black dots and the subject also wears body chains, armlets and bracelets, all indicated by red paint. There is black pigment on the pubic triangle.

Figures such as this have often been identified as 'dolls'. The nakedness, prominent pubic triangle, swollen breasts and stomach, however, suggest that such representations are more likely to have been linked to fertility, either during life or as part of the regeneration of the deceased. Indeed many examples have been found in tombs of women, men and children suggesting that they are closely linked to rebirth in the afterlife. It is possible that such figures were intended to function as votives to gods such as Min or Hathor who were directly associated with fertility.

This example is typical of the New Kingdom form, which had been established in the Middle Kingdom. These early fertility figures were more schematic than their later counterparts and by the Roman period the type becomes combined with the so-called offerant or orantes figures (see cat. 89-90). A similar piece, now in the Petrie Museum of Egyptian Archaeology (UC 16760) has an additional strip of clay intended to represent hair over the proper left side of the face and an additional disk of clay on the forehead.

Compare: Petrie Illahun Kahun and Gurob 1891: 19 pl. XIX.43

92 Clay amulet in the form of a woman giving birth

Height 5.2 cm
Second century BC to first century AD
Antinoe
Given by the Egypt Exploration Fund
E.104.1914

Nile silt clay, mould-made in two halves and joined. The two legs are broken, and the left arm, that would have once held onto the left thigh is also damaged, otherwise the piece in intact. There are traces of plaster on the surface, and red pigment on the breasts and legs.

The figure is that of a naked female, sitting with her legs splayed. Her stomach is swollen suggesting pregnancy and she holds her lower abdomen with her right hand. Her head is cast downwards and rests on her right shoulder as if in exhaustion or pain. The back is roughly modelled, with a small suspension hole at the back, suggesting that the figure may have functioned as an amulet.

Such figures are described as images of *Baubo*, who was a goddess of childbirth and fertility. In the Greek and Roman world the goddess is associated with the rites of Demeter. In Egypt such figures frequently occur wearing the wig of the goddess Hathor. Later they become associated with Isis. One particular area in eastern Alexandria was called Eleusis, after the principal mainland Greek sanctuary of Demeter. Like the older city, Alexandria held a festival called the Eleusinian mysteries. It has been suggested (Török 1995: 130-31 and Fraser 1972: 199) that such images may well have been directly associated with these festivals in the city. However, it seems likely that they were found throughout Egypt, wherever this particular cult was celebrated or more generally for women in childbirth. Both of the Fitzwilliam Museum's figures (cat. 93) are thought to have come from Antinoe. They arrived in the Museum as part of the Egypt Exploration Fund's gifts to supporting institutions.

The hook on the back of this figure suggests that it was used as a amulet or charm. It is slightly larger than the usual size for wearing around the neck. However, it is possible that it was hung up in the home, or perhaps even dedicated in order to ensure a safe labour for the woman involved.

The number of examples found suggests that such figures were popular. Although Egyptian in origin they remained common in the Ptolemaic and Roman periods. The solid core suggests a Ptolemaic rather than Roman date for this particular piece. Parallel examples are dated from the second century BC (Török 1995: 132-33). Solid mould-made terracottas were also made by Egyptian craftsmen (Ashton 2003: 72-77).

Compare: Dunand 1990: 205-07 no. 561-65; Török 1995: 130-31 no. 181-89.

93 Terracotta rattle in the form of a woman giving birth

Height 7.1 cm
First to early second century AD
Antinoe
Given by the Egypt Exploration Fund
E.86.1914

Mould-made terracotta figure, manufactured in two halves. The clay is Nile silt. The face of the subject is damaged and there are firing cracks at the top of the thighs.

This little terracotta figure seems to have functioned as a rattle; there are one or two clay pellets inside. Some such objects seem to have been used as toys, but the form of the Fitzwilliam Museum's rattle suggests it served a religious rather than frivolous function.

The figure is positioned with her legs in the air; the left is held back at the thigh. Her swollen stomach suggests that she is pregnant and her right hand is positioned on her lower abdomen as if waiting for the birth. The pendulous breasts are probably a reference to fertility and appear on many traditional Egyptian gods connected with childbirth.

The woman's face is rounded and almost caricature-like in its features. Her hair is parted down the centre and pulled back into a bun. On her head is a garland suggesting a festival connection. The naturalistic hairstyle suggests a date early in the Roman period. The back of the piece is well modelled, with the hair, rounded back and buttock cheeks retouched after the initial moulding of the figure.

At the top of the back of the head is a small hole, with some wear-marks suggesting that the rattle was attached to the end of a stick. In its form the rattle is nothing like the Egyptian sistrum, which is traditionally decorated with a Hathor head or deity during this period. The basic meaning and references to fertility, however, remain the same.

Animal Cults

94 Limestone bowl with a crocodile

Width 8.1 cm
First century AD
Provenance unknown, Egypt
Bequeathed by R.G. Gayer-Anderson
E.GA.587.1947

The exterior is carved as if in the form of a shell and the interior is slightly concave. The crocodile and bowl are abraded on the high points and there is extensive surface scratching.

Carved into the lower section of the inner wall is a single crocodile, its tail twisted up to echo the shape of the vessel. The head is lifted slightly to indicate movement. Limestone versions of these vessels are unusual, although they are relatively common in steatite. There is no spout, as on the steatite versions (cat. 69-70) but there are parallels in this stone featuring crocodiles.

In addition to representing the god Sobek, crocodiles had different associations in different parts of Egypt, as explained by Herodotos, a Greek historian of the fifth century BC. Herodotos mentions the treatment of these animals in *Histories* Book II, chapters 69-70:

'Some of the Egyptians consider crocodiles sacred; others do not, but treat them as enemies. Those who live near Thebes and Lake Moeris consider them very sacred. Every household raises one crocodile, trained to be tame; they put ornaments of glass and gold on its ears and bracelets on its forefeet, provide special food and offerings for it, and give the creatures the best of treatment while they live; after death, the crocodiles are embalmed and buried in sacred coffins. But around Elephantine they are not held sacred, and are even eaten. The Egyptians do not call them crocodiles, but khampsae. The Ionians named them crocodiles, from their resemblance to the lizards, which they have in their walls. There are many different ways of crocodile hunting; I will write of the way that I think most worth mentioning. The hunter baits a hook with a hog's back, and lets it float into the midst of the river; he himself stays on the bank with a young live pig, which he beats. Hearing the squeals of the pig, the crocodile goes after the sound, and meets the bait, which it swallows; then the hunters pull the line. When the crocodile is drawn ashore, first of all the hunter smears its eyes over with mud; when this is done, the quarry is very easily mastered -- no light matter, without that'.

95 Fake crocodile Mummy

Length 32 cm
First century BC-AD
Provenance unkown, Egypt.
Transferred from the Museum of Zoology, Cambridge
E.I.1894

The 'animal' is carefully wrapped in linen with an intricate three-panel design across the body. The eyes were added separately and stitched onto the head. A branch has been inserted to form the nose and mouth of the animal.

Animal cults were extremely popular in the late periods of Egyptian history and their appeal continued into the Roman period. Throughout Egypt vast cemeteries of mummified animals were places of pilgrimage. In addition to the cemeteries of more identifiable animals such as the Apis, Mnervis and Buchis bulls, who were all considered personifications of gods (cat. 99), there were burial sites for a variety of 'mortal' animals, often of the type associated with a specific deity. X-rays have shown that many animals were culled for the purpose of providing bodies to dedicate at the sites and it seems as if the schemes offered a profit to temples and the priests who bred them. The bodies of the animals were then placed in wooden coffins or simple pottery vessels and buried within catacombs along with votive offerings.

Some mummies within the Fitzwilliam Museum's collections contain the bones of more than one animal, others a single bone. An X-ray of this particular crocodile shows that it consists of stones and possible pot sherds (as indicated by the very thin masses towards the head end). It would seem that fake mummies were a widespread problem during ancient times. Ptolemy V issued a royal decree stating that each container (cat. 96) that was bought should contain one animal, suggesting that pilgrims were regularly cheated.

Further reading: Égypte Romaine 1997: 168-69 no. 197-201.

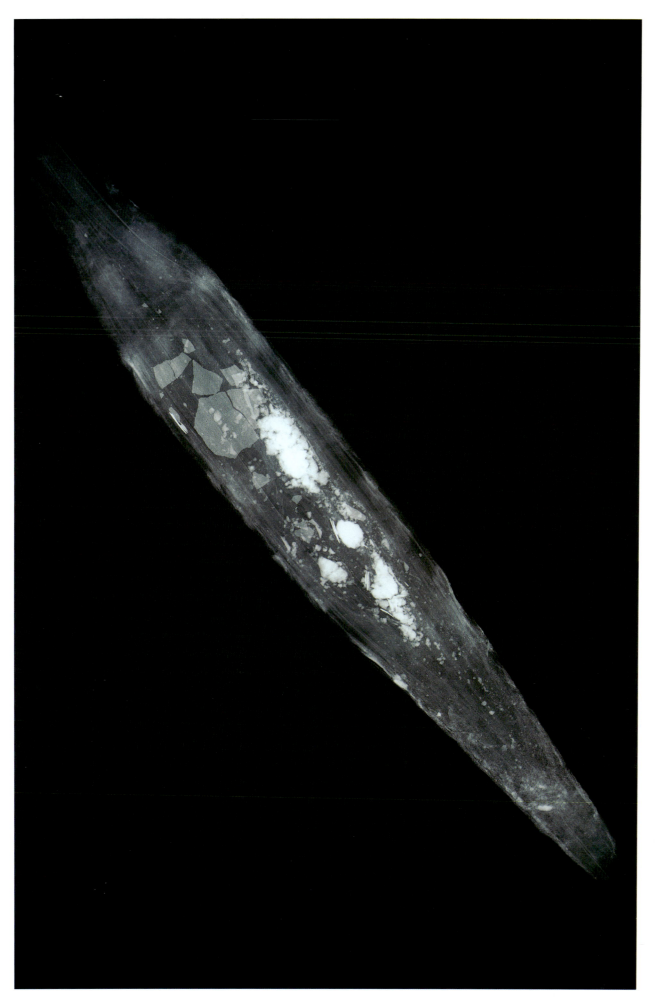

96 Copper alloy statue of a cat

Height 37 cm
Second century AD
Provenance unknown
Bequeathed by Charles Brinsley Marlay
E.4.1912

Hollow copper alloy figure in the form of a seated cat, cast in one piece. The object was cast upside down as indicated by the tang which may well have resulted from the metal solidifying in a sprue (channel) in the mould during the manufacturing process. The base is open to reveal that most of the core has been cleaned out of the figure with the exception of the nose region. The legs are also solid cast. X-rays reveal the presence of a number of iron core pins are present including one at the top of the nose and one at the top of the head; there are a number of others within the body. The eyes are made of glass with what appears to be foil inserted at the back in order to form the pupils. The entire body is covered in a pattern that most likely was cast from the wax and which represents fur. Further details were added by incised decoration in the form of a rope-like necklace supporting a wedjat eye, which is placed over the left pectoral, and also a scarab and eye on the top of the cat's head. These last two motifs were associated with the sun god Ra.

Large scale statuettes such as this were common in the Late and Ptolemaic periods and continued to be manufactured in Roman Egypt. Many served as coffins to mummified cats. The Fitzwilliam Museum's example has a tang at the front and would have been placed upon a wooden or copper alloy base, which may have formed part of the lid for the coffin of a mummified cat. Other mummified cats were wrapped and then placed in a pottery or wooden coffin.

Not until the Third Intermediate period did the common cat become associated with the goddess Bastet. The appearance of the more traditional representations of the goddess (cat. 97) alongside statues such as this suggests that the two facets were seen to be separate.

Many cats were buried at the Sacred Animal necropolis at Saqqara and several examples of large-scale Copper alloy cats have been found there. Some examples with bases/lids still intact have nonsense hieroglyphs decorating the sides as a form of mock dedication. This would suggest a wider tourist industry of buying and dedicating such objects, rather than one that simply involved the priests, whom one would expect to have been able to write competently in hieroglyphs, at least during the first three centuries AD.

Further reading: Malek 1997.

97 Silver statuette of Bastet

Height of figure 8.1 cm
First to third centuries AD
Provenance unknown, Egypt
Bought from Sir William Matthew Flinders Petrie
E.20.1900

Solid cast silver figure, originally attached to a base, now missing. The nose has been rubbed and shines as a result.

The figure is a standing representation of a cat-headed female figure and can be identified as the goddess Bastet, whose main cult centre was Bubastis in the Egyptian Delta and there was also a large temple to the goddess at Saqqara. Silver figures of this size are not common; most are substantially smaller, about half of the size of the Fitzwilliam Museum's statuette. Although this form was particularly common in the Late and Ptolemaic periods, certain features of this particular example that deviate from the original forms indicate it is Roman in date.

The form of dress that the goddess wears is stylised and whereas on Ptolemaic examples the decorative lines are carefully incised to form a delicate pattern on a flat garment, here they produce folds. It is likely that this pattern was cast from the wax; it is possible that additional details were then chased into the metal. The way in which the goddess also holds the *situla* (vessel) over her forearm is also common during the Roman period. In her left arm she holds what appears to be an *aegis* decorated with the head of a cat wearing a sun disk crown. Both features were copied from earlier figures. In the cat's right hand, however, is not the usual *sistrum* (rattle). Instead the goddess holds a loop-like object that is larger than one would typically expect for a rattle and is without the necessary struts that would make a real version work. Although flail-like in appearance we must assume that the artist has remained true to the established form and that the rattle was simply left unfinished. Unlike the more usual human hands the cat appears to have paws. Her feet are, as to be expected, human in form. On some Roman versions she is shown with sandals.

The figure was bought from Sir William Matthew Flinders Petrie. The modern marble base on which the figure stood when it came to the Fitzwilliam Museum is one of a consignment that Petrie bought and used to display such objects: there are many examples in the Petrie Museum of Egyptian Archaeology, London. There is no indication of where the statue was found. It is likely that Petrie collected or bought it on account of its unusual features: such peculiarities seem to have fascinated the Egyptologist, who was passionately interested in all periods of Egyptian history and culture. Sadly, many such pieces are dismissed as forgeries.

In ancient Egyptian religion there were two feline goddesses: the lion-headed Sekhmet and Bastet, who resembled the domestic cat. The two represented different aspects. Sekhmet was the aggressive and powerful feline who rampaged in the eastern desert whereas Bastet was the more calming aspect of the cat family.

Further reading: Langton 1940; Malek 1997.

98 Faience figure of a Ram

Height 18 cm, Length 27.5 cm
First century AD
Provenance unknown, Egypt
Bequeathed by Arnold John Hugh Smith
E.6.1964

Broken and repaired in several places along the back and neck. Four large clay circles on the base are the remains of the cones used to stack or support the object during the firing process (Ashton 2003: 42-43).

Mould-made figure of a ram probably manufactured in two halves and then joined. The base is sealed with an added slab of faience. The figure is hollow with a hole for air that has simply been made by pushing an implement into the unfired base. The glaze is blue-green in colour and has been either painted onto the surface or simply dipped. There are patches where the core shows through and also visible drip marks down the sides of the figure, particularly between the legs.

Rams could represent a number of deities. They are traditionally linked to the god Khnum in Egypt but could also be associated with local gods such as the Ram of Mendes. Amun was associated with the ram and this connection was shown in the selection of attributes for the Greek Ammon, who is shown with ram's horns (cat. 53). It seems likely therefore that the Fitzwilliam ram was intended to represent a deity and was perhaps offered as a votive or used as an effigy of a god. Figurines of this size are rare and in fact most faience figurines from the Late and Ptolemaic periods are substantially smaller. Several sections of a similar woolly coat rendered in faience were found by Petrie when he excavated the faience kilns at Kom Helul in Memphis (Ashton 2003: 57), suggesting that there may be a link between this piece and the site. The many fragments from Kom Helul of the similar proportions suggest, however, that this figure was not unique and others may well have been manufactured from the same mould.

Further reading: Ashton 2003: 39-58.

99 Terracotta figure in the form of a bust of a bull

Height 14.6 cm
First century AD
Memphis
Given by the British School of Archaeology in Egypt
E.18.1913

Nile silt clay, mould-made in two halves; the back is unmodelled. The surface is worn and some of the features are difficult to distinguish, suggesting that this came from a mould that had been used on several occasions prior to the manufacture of this particular piece. Red and black pigment is preserved on the surface, along with patches of the plaster wash that would once have covered the entire figurine as a base for the painted decoration. There are finger marks on both sides of the inner surface where the artist has pushed the clay into the mould. There is also some waste clay that has adhered to the outside surface around the bull's crown and horns.

The bull wears a sun-disk and *uraeus* between the horns. It appears as if some kind of amulet and necklace is intended around the neck and resting on the chest.

The bull could represent one of three deities: Apis (who was the embodiment of the god Ptah at Memphis), Mnevis (who was the embodiment of the god Re at Heliopolis) or Buchis (who was believed to the embodiment of Re and Osiris at Armant).

Each bull had to have specific markings, and although those associated with the chosen incarnation were also divine by association, searches were undertaken throughout the land for a replacement when a bull died. The Apis bull needed especially complex markings: it had to be black with a vulture on its back, a white lozenge on its forehead and a scarab-shaped mark under its tongue. Mnevis was black with tufts of hair on its body and tail. Buchis had to posses a white body and black face.

This particular figure is likely to represent Apis on account of its Memphite provenance. Strabo, writing in the first century, (*Geographies* 17.1.31) describes viewing the Apis bull at Memphis in some detail: 'In front of the sanctuary is a courtyard, in which there is another sanctuary for the mother of the bull. Into this court they set Apis free at a certain hour, especially so that foreigners can see him. For, although people can see him through the window of the sanctuary they want to see him outside as well. When he has finished a short bout of skipping in the courtyard they take him back into his familiar stall'.

Compare: Fjeldhagen (1995) 176-77, no's. 172-74.

Further reading: Thompson 1988: 271 and 273-5 (for Apis in the Roman period); Ashton 2003: 6-7 and 9.

100. Copper alloy diobol of Domitian (AD 81-96)

Diameter 24 mm
Weight 7.81 g
AD 85/86
Alexandria mint
CM.46-1943

Obv. Laureate head of the Emperor Domitian facing right. Accompanied by the Greek legend: ΑVΤ ΚΑΙΣΑΡ ΔΟΜΙΤΙΑΝΟΣ ΣΕΒ ΓΕΡΜ.

Rev. Apis bull standing towards the right, with sun-disk between its horns. In front of the bull is an altar or offering table.

Many Emperors shared a close relationship with the Apis bulls and the priesthood at Memphis. When a bull died a costly burial ensued, which was often supported by the ruler.

Above the bull is the date LE = year 5 of Domitian's regnal dating.

Dattari 576

101. Billon tetradrachm of Hadrian (AD 117-138)

Diameter 23.9 mm
Weight 12.73 g
AD 119/120
Alexandria mint
CM.58-1943

Obv. Laureate bust of Hadrian facing right, with drapery on left shoulder. Accompanied by the Greek legend: ΑVΤ ΚΑΙ ΤΡΑΙ-ΑΔΡΙΑ ϹΕΒ.

Rev. Hippopotamus facing right. In Egypt the hippopotamus represented the god Seth, who killed and mutilated his brother Osiris. On temple reliefs of the Ptolemaic and Roman periods Seth in the form of a hippopotamus is often speared by Horus, who thus avenges his father. In Rome and to Roman viewers the hippopotamus was simply a symbol of Egypt and often an animal who was hunted and is thus shown on wall paintings and mosaics.

In the field above the hippopotamus is the date LΔ = year 4 of Hadrian's regnal dating.

Milne 959

When in Rome...

Although it is easy to categorise Egyptian culture in Rome as 'Egyptomania' there were important developments, such as the changes in the representation of Isis, which appear to have taken place there. Official buildings, sanctuaries and public areas were decorated with Egyptian material that had been imported from Egypt, and the legacy of Egyptian culture that remained in Rome offered easy access for later generations without having to visit Africa (Ziegler 1994: 16). Objects were imported, copied, interpreted and then exported back to their place of origin, forming a complex system of cultural exchange; and in addition to supplying grain, Egypt supplied stone from its quarries for buildings that were Roman in form, but which may have hinted at the east by their unusual appearance.

It is often the use of Egyptian and Egyptianising objects in Italy that is unorthodox, although in many cases it appears that the emperors may well have been advised by Egyptians. Were the obelisks that stood in front of Augustus' mausoleum simply there for propaganda, or had the emperor be been told of their true function? Did Gaius Cestius, whose pyramid, built before 12 BC, still stands today in an area named after it, (see fig. on p. 4) believe that it would enhance his passage to the next life? We may never know and indeed their reasons may be numerous. What we can conclude, however, is that Egyptian culture flourished in Rome and Italy and was in many respects appropriated to form a class of objects that was different to those found in the province but which were certainly closer to our own interpretation of Egypt. In many respects the Roman view of Egypt is similar to that of Europe today and as such offers us an easy passage into a vast and complex society and culture.

102 Marble statue in the form of a bust of Serapis

Height 22 cm
Second century AD
Provenance unknown, probably Italy
Given by Dr John Disney
GR.15.1850

This marble bust shows a classic Roman Serapis, which is often erroneously linked with the Alexandrian original. The *modius* (corn measure) is decorated with foliage, stressing the fertility of the god; the locks of hair on the forehead and the divided beard distinguish the god from other similar deities and both become strong features that are adopted by Roman Emperors in the third century AD to associate them with the god (see cat. 18).

In this form the statue is unlikely to have served a cultic purpose and was conceivably part of a decorative group, perhaps including Isis. The changes to the god's image are recorded on oil lamps dating to the reign of the Emperor Domitian towards the end of the first century AD (Ashton 2003: 34). The god appears on Roman Imperial coinage from Egypt in this bust form (cat. 13 and 17) sometimes with his consort Isis, who enjoyed a similar change of iconography and popularity in the Roman world.

103 Marble statue of the god Bes

Height 59.5 cm
Second to mid-third century AD
From Rome, formerly in the Palazzo Verospi
Given by A. E. Gregory
GR.1.1818

Parts of the forehead, nose mouth and hands/knees are restored.

In addition to cult statues of Egyptian deities the Romans also used their images for decorative purposes, often in sanctuaries dedicated to Egyptian cults. The Fitzwilliam Museum's statue of the god Bes is in fact a functioning fountain, which allowed water to pour through the lion's mouth carved onto the base of the statue.

Here Bes, originally a god linked to the protection of children and pregnant women, is shown in a squatting pose, his genitalia resting on the surface between his feet. He is identifiable here from his dwarf-like proportions, leonine beard and exaggerated face, and from the animal skin (usually that of a panther) that he wears around his shoulders. Certain features that appear on the original Egyptian Bes figurines that are missing from this Roman example: namely the plumed crown, and the prominent leonine ears. Two further Romanised features are the animal-headed amulet, apparently wolf, and the bead-like belt that he wears (Vassilika 1998: 106).

Although Bes often appears to be squatting on Egyptian representations, he is rarely seated in this manner. This pose, along with the use of the god's image for a fountain, means that the statue is Egyptianising rather than true to the Egyptian form. The style is accentuated by the use of a Greek marble as a medium. The deeply carved iris and pupil of the eyes suggest a date between the mid second and mid third centuries AD.

Vassilika 1998: 106-07 no. 51.

Further reading: Roullet 1972: 88-89.

104 Hard stone statue of a bound captive

Height 35 cm
Second century AD
Provenance unknown, probably Italy. Formerly in the collection of Josette Day Solvoy, Paris.
Tomasso Brothers' Private Collection. The statue was sold at auction in Paris in December 2002 and had formerly been part of the collection of French film actress Josette Day Solvoy (1914-1978).

The stone is probably meta-dolorite, a coarse-grained metamorphosed rock of basaltic composition. The statue is preserved from the thighs to the neck. There is some superficial damage to the surface, particularly at the breaks around the legs and the neck. The surface at the break of the legs is roughly chiselled perhaps suggesting piecing of the stone. The head has been removed to reveal a smooth almost polished surface.

The subject is male and has a youthful but unathletic body. There are signs of excess fat at the sides of the torso and around the top of the chest. The stomach is slightly rounded in profile accentuating the awkwardness of the pose. The arms are positioned behind his lower back, right over left and bound by a rope that is wrapped around the wrists. The shoulders are slightly rounded and the subject appears to be standing with his weight on his right leg with the left leg positioned slightly forwards. Unlike the captives on the Hawara foot-case (cat. 81), it is unlikely for practical reasons that this statue stood on one leg.

The figure wears a loose fitting short kilt with folds of drapery apparently rumpled by the position of his arms and his stance. The wig or hair is stylised in form with an upturned curls resting on each shoulder and a rectangular section between, perhaps unfinished or mis-interpreted by the artist. This hairstyle identifies the subject as a Libyan and the statue is intended as a version of the traditional bound foreign captive (cat. 79).

It is highly likely that this statue was one of a pair of bound captives and feasible that the second was either a Nubian or an Asiatic. The two may well have decorated a doorway of a private or imperial villa. Such captives would have had a particular relevance for an Emperor, whose role it was to quash the foreign foes of Egypt.

Several statues from Italy, including portraits of Roman Emperors were executed in this particular stone but few statues in this stone have been found in Egypt, (Belli Pasqua 1995). A colossal infant Hercules, now in the Capitoline Museums, Rome (Belli Pasqua 1995: 99 no. 56 pl. LXI) is testimony to the use of this material by Roman artists and also to its popularity. Sphinxes are particularly common in this stone, with examples preserved in the Egyptian Museum, Munich (Grimm et al. 2003: 103-06) and Villa Borghese, Rome. There is also the aforementioned (cat. 36) Osiris-Canopus jar in the Vatican Museums. Unfortunately, none of the pieces has a certain provenance, although some have been linked to Hadrian's Villa outside Rome (Raeder 1983 for discussion and earlier bibliography). Most of these green hard stone statues have been dated to the first and second centuries AD, and it is possible that many of the Romano-Egyptian statues in this stone formed part of a single original group.

The subject and stone evoke an Egyptian theme and it is likely that the original owner of the statue was interested in Egyptian culture. It is obvious to see how the half-naked torso would appeal to Roman imperial tastes and the statue is testimony to the skill of the artist who carved it. This is the first time that the piece has been displayed and published, and it is hoped that its pair or indeed the missing head may well surface as a result. Many Romano-Egyptian and Egyptianising pieces have been misinterpreted as modern copies of Egyptian sculpture and as a result it can be difficult for those new to the field to determine when a statue is a Roman copy and when it is modern (Ashton 2002).

Romano-Egyptian or Egyptianising?

The question over whether the statue falls within the classical or Egyptian traditions is not easily decided. As mentioned above statues were executed in this stone in both traditions. The stone suggests that the artist intended the piece to be linked with Egypt, but during the second century AD many coloured stones were utilised by Roman artists. In terms of its form, it is without a back pillar, but this particular attribute does not feature on representations of bound captives in the Old Kingdom. The very nature of the bound-captive subject does not lend itself to the use of a back pillar, so that this form of statue had its own particular tradition. This statue cannot therefore automatically be placed within the classical or Egyptianising repertoire. There are features, such as the wig, which are similar to Egyptian depictions. The naturalistic kilt, however, sits more comfortably within the classical and so Egyptianising sphere.

105 Hard stone Roman copy of a statue of a Ptolemaic queen

Height 85 cm
Second century AD
Probably from Hadrian's Villa, Rome
Tomasso Brothers' Private Collection, formerly Harrington House Collection, Lincolnshire.

*The stone is probably meta-dolorite, a coarse-grained metamorphosed rock of basaltic composition. There is a crack running through the base and some surface damage to the front. The proper left shoulder and back of the headdress have been repaired, but were probably originally pieced in antiquity. The right arm has been broken at the elbow and wrist and repaired.

Striding female figure with left leg forwards in traditional Egyptian stance. The statue has an inscribed back pillar with a roughly finished surface; it ends at the base of head, thus placing the statue firmly within the Egyptian repertoire. Certain stylistic features such as the modelling of the face and the stylised lotus (?) on the brow are, however, typical of the Roman period.

The voluptuous figure with swollen abdomen, perhaps an indication of fertility, is also typical of statues from the Ptolemaic period and indicates a strong connection of style. The subject wears a sheath-like translucent dress, as indicated by the hem directly above the ankles. The headdress is in the traditional tri-partite form but the lappets are thinner than those of the Ptolemaic period, revealing a further Roman feature. The statue is therefore a Roman-Egyptian copy of a Ptolemaic original.

fig. 9

The subject holds her right arm by her side and in her hand, rather than the usual bar, she holds a cloth. This attribute is found on statues dating to the eighteenth and nineteenth dynasties, particularly royal women (fig. 9), and it appears later on a twenty-fifth dynasty statue of the consort Shepenwepet, now in the Egyptian Museum, Cairo. A similar cloth also appears on two statues now in the Vatican Museums, one a Ptolemaic original of Arsinoe II, sister and wife of Ptolemy II, and the other a Roman copy of the statue of Arsinoe II on an original Ptolemaic base (Ashton 2003b: 149 and in McFarlane and Morgan eds. Forthcoming). On the original the right arm has been replaced and is made in the same stone as the copy. It seems likely, therefore, that the same artist or workshop created the arm on the original and the copy, and had some reason to show a cloth rather than bar: presumably the feature was copied from another statue. On the Tomasso Brother's statue the left hand is drawn across the upper abdomen and holds the handle of what was perhaps intended to represent a sistrum (rattle). This same feature also recurs on both the Vatican representations, which probably acted as models for the Tomasso Brothers' statue.

A missing statue from Hadrian's Villa?

In May 2000 the contents of Harrington House in Lincolnshire were sold at auction. Amongst the objects was a statue that was described in the sale catalogue as a late-nineteenth or early-twentieth century copy of an original dating to the third century BC. And so, like many

Romano-Egyptian pieces it had been classified as modern (Ashton 2002). In the summer of 2001 the new owners brought the statue to London in order to have it examined. They had recently seen a special exhibition on Cleopatra, organised by the British Museum, and quite rightly noted that many of the pieces on display were similar to their own statue. Many such pieces served a decorative purpose in cult centres and villas in Italy and in Egypt too such representations continued to be made.

The closest parallels for the use of this stone and the form of statue come from Italy. Research on the piece revealed a drawing from a book, *Alticchiero*, published in 1787 by Justine Wynne, Countess Orsini-Rosenberg. The book is a description of the villa of this name, outside Padua in northern Italy. The drawing has a scale, which accords with the height of the statue; it also shows the same unusual headdress and styling of the lappets of the wig. As the pose of the statue in the drawing is also identical to that of the statue it can be identified as the same. Justine Wynne was half Greek on her mother's side, but spent time in Venice as well as London in order to bring up her children in the Catholic faith. As a very young woman she had been a lover of the famous Casanova. In 1739 she had married Sir Richard Wynne and following his death in 1751 she became the wife of Count Orsini-Rosenberg, an Austrian ambassador in Venice. Her book states that the statue of 'Isis' was from Hadrian's Villa. It is one of two ancient Egyptian objects illustrated from the Villa's gardens, the other being a seated scribe. The fact that the statue is a copy of a colossal pair of images of Arsinoe II that were themselves possibly brought to Rome by the Emperor Hadrian and which were placed in imperial gardens in Rome, suggests that the image was one that was known to the Emperor.

It is likely that in antiquity the statue was originally one of a pair. In Roullet's 1972 publication on Egyptian and Egyptianising monuments of Imperial Rome, there is a drawing of a fragment of a second female statue, which to my knowledge has not yet been found. This statue seems to have the same wig as the Alticchiero queen and a lotus-like symbol on her brow (Ashton forthcoming). Such representations were often in pairs; one of which strides forward onto the right foot rather than the more usual left.

The alleged connection with Hadrian's Villa is supported by the existence of several other statues, now housed in the Vatican Museums, manufactured in the same stone and with similar features (Ashton in McFarlane and Morgan eds. Forthcoming; and forthcoming 2006). Some are originals, others copies of original pieces. The provenance of many Romano-Egyptian statues will remain questionable, but it is certain that the Alticchiero queen can be dated to the Hadrianic period by stylistic comparison with other pieces with a secure provenance. A recent study of the Egyptian sculptural programme at Hadrian's Villa has revealed a series of carefully planned and executed themes (Ashton forthcoming 2006). Many of these served the cult of Antinous but others showed an appreciation of Egyptian art. A copy of a Ptolemaic statue would have been the perfect combination of cultures for this particular Emperor, who was well known for his keen interest in Greece. Until recently Hadrian's patronage of Egyptian cults has received relatively little attention, but the manufacture of images such as this during his reign illustrates that Romano-Egyptian culture thrived.

Furthermore, the Tomasso Brothers' statue has little in common with eighteenth century copies of Egyptian sculpture. A comparison with "Egyptiansing" decorative sculpture from this period, where the modelling and stances are more fluid than even those of Roman period, shows that the Tomasso Brothers' statue is neither the usual proportions, nor with the same modelling as modern copies. Compare for example the red Egyptian marble set by Giuseppe Valadier (1762-1839) as illustrated in the exhibition catalogue Charles-Gaffiot and H. Lavagne eds. 1999: 336, cat. 183. Nor does the statue reveal any concessions to the classical form as with many late eighteenth-century Egyptianising sculptures (cat. 109). Humbert et al. eds. (1994: 269-71 no. 154-55) illustrate two statues of Antinous attributed to Pierre-Nicolas Beauvallet, which show a hybrid of Roman Egyptianising and Egyptian forms, like cat. 109 the hands are positioned away from the body but unlike cat. 109 the left and right legs of each stride forward. Even on Egyptianising statues dating to the late eighteenth century that include a back pillar, such as those by Antoine-Guillaume Grandjacquet (Pantazzi in Humbert et al eds. 1994: 101-103 no. 39-40) the hands adopt a more naturalistic position on the statue of Isis, and on the Osiris puntelli hold the wrists away from the legs. These are subtle but substantial differences that allow the modern viewer to distinguish between statues of the eighteenth century and those that of Roman in date.

Further Reading: Orsini-Rosenberg 1787; Roullet 1972; Humbert, Pantazzi and Ziegler eds. 1994.

106 Porphyry funerary urn

Height 33cm
Second to fourth centuries AD
Provenance unknown, Italy.
Private Collection, The Tomasso Brothers

There is a small chip in the rim of the vessel and the handle is of a different stone and has been added as a separate piece, possibly in antiquity or in the eighteenth/nineteenth centuries. The form and carving appears to be ancient (compare Malgouyres 2003: 55) and it is sympathetic to the piece, echoing the clean lines of the vessel and lid.

The vessel is carved from a single block of porphyry and is carefully finished at the bottom with a single circle surrounding a central dot. Concentric circles form an outer base imitating metal and ceramic vessels. This part of the vase would have been carved with a lathe and it is likely that the core of the original was drilled out to form a hollow. The lid is made from the same vein of stone and imitates the base. An outer ridge allows the lid to sit comfortably onto the lip of the main vessel and then a series of three concentric circles break up the space between the outer and inner edges.

Porphyry was a popular stone in Imperial Rome and was utilised for statues, vessels and architectural elements throughout Italy and Egypt. Especially notable are vessels that were connected to Egyptian sanctuaries or forms of Romano-Egyptian vessel. One particularly well-executed piece is preserved at the Museum of the Sanctuary of Isis at Benevento. A large snake is coiled on top of plain cylindrical vase, similar in form to the vase under discussion here, but squatter. Such vessels were part of Egyptian cults and perhaps also the temple decoration, invoking Egypt by means of the stone.

Further reading: Malgouyres 2003:46-47 no. 4 (a Canopic jar?) and 54-56 no. 9 (a more elaborate and squatter form of funerary urn, but with shared features).

107 Porphyry column

Height 135 cm, Upper diameter 22.5 cm
Second century AD
Provenance unknown, probably Italy
GR.29.1869

The base is uneven and a section is missing, with the result that the column stands at a slight angle. There are dents in the surface and some missing sections that have been pieced with porphyry of a different grain. Both the top and bottom surfaces are roughly finished with chisel marks clearly visible, suggesting that the column probably served an architectural function.

The shaft is plain with the exception of a single ridge around the upper section and a ledge at the lower end, giving the impression of a base block. It is possible that the substantial dent in the upper section on one side may have supported a decorative motif, now missing. A similar, although larger, pair of columns are decorated with portrait busts of the Emperors Trajan and Nerva (Malgouyres 2003: 51). Many such columns were re-used in churches and palaces (Malgouyres 2003: 52-53 fig. 18) showing the lasting appeal of the stone and simple architectural forms that the Roman columns were made in.

It is probable that the Fitzwilliam Museum's column shaft was once part of an architectural scheme, its size suggests that it might have served a decorative rather than structural purpose, perhaps in the upper part of a building.

Compare Malgouyres 2003: 51-54 no. 7-8.

Further reading: Maxfield and Peacock 2001.

108 Fragment of a marble statue of Antinous

Height 41 cm
Second century AD (AD 130-137)
From Hadrian's Villa at Tivoli (near Rome)
Formerly the Collection of the Marquis of Lansdowne, Bequeathed by C.S. Rickets and C.H. Shannon
GR.100.1937

The nose, upper lip, chin and bust are eighteenth-century restorations in stone. There is plaster fill on the right cheek and some of the leaves of the crown have been restored with plaster, others in stone. There are traces of iron corrosion products on the headdress associated with old attachments. Originally the portrait would have been part of an over-lifesized classical statue.

In AD 130 the Emperor Hadrian arrived in Egypt with a party of family and friends. The group visited Alexandria, which had just suffered unrest and rebellion, before heading out to the Western Desert in search of a lion that had terrorised travellers for some time. Accompanying Hadrian was his young lover Antinous, who was around twenty years of age. The pair set off into the desert to hunt the lion, but Antinous was caught by the beast and had to be rescued by the Emperor. This event was celebrated on an arch in Rome and quite possibly on a relief from Hadrian's Villa (Ashton forthcoming 2006), placing Hadrian within a mythological context.

Antinous' fortunes, however, did not improve during the remainder of the trip. As Hadrian and his entourage set sail up the Nile towards Upper Egypt a tragedy occurred: Antinous fell into the river and drowned. The Emperor was devastated and the literary sources record that he 'cried like a woman'. Several questions surrounded the death and even in antiquity rumours of sacrifice surfaced. It was thought that Antinous might have died in order to save the Emperor's failing health. Modern historians have also suggested that other members of the Imperial party might have murdered Antinous, concerned about the amount of influence that the youth held. This particular suggestion seems unlikely because there is no evidence that Antinous had political aspirations. It is more probable either that he sacrificed himself or that he simply suffered an accidental death. We will probably never know the full circumstances surrounding the death of Antinous, but his subsequent deification is well documented in both the written and archaeological records.

In death Antinous became Osiris Antinous, and as such was worshipped as the Dead Antinous, similar in many respects to the aforementioned cult of Osiris-Apis (cat. 19). His cult statues showed the youth in the guise of an Egyptian king, wearing a *nemes* headcloth, sometimes with the royal or divine *uraeus*, and wearing the Egyptian kilt (cat. 109). The Fitzwilliam Museum's Antinous shows the youth in the guise of the Greek equivalent of Osiris- the god of wine and also the underworld, Dionysos. As such the statue shows Antinous wearing a crown of ivy leaves and grapes. It is one of several known images of the youth as the god. He also appears as Hermes and Apollo. Following his death many divine statues were re-cut with the portrait features of Antinous, resulting in a mixed iconography that may not have been intended from outset. The Dionysos and Egyptian Osiris types seem, however, to have been intended links with divinity.

Vassilika 1998: 114-15 no. 55.

Further reading:, Clairmont 1966; Birley 1997; Lambert 1997; Ashton forthcoming 2006.

109 Tin-glazed earthenware statues of Osiris-Antinous

Height 117.5 cm
Late eighteenth century
Made in Italy or France
C. 2388 A & B

One of the statues has a substantial break across the middle and both have suffered some surface damage. There is an air hole in the back of each statue for firing.

The statues are the same in form. The two form a pair and are a hybrid of Roman statues of Osiris-Antinous, or the Dead Antinous. They show a male figure wearing a striated kilt with a low slung belt resting below the abdomen. In each hand is a so-called enigmatic bar (enigmatic because we are not certain of its meaning): it has been suggested that it might represent the staff held by Egyptian officials or simply be a space filler. This attribute is commonly found on Egyptian statuary from the Old Kingdom onwards. Interestingly many of the Roman statues deviate from this tradition by representing either a bag or a folded cloth in the hands. Here the modern artist has maintained the traditional form. There are, however, features that deviate from even Roman copies of Egyptian statuary, namely the lock of hair that has replaced the traditional 'pigtail' at the back of the *nemes* headcloth. The ribbed decoration on the *nemes* also forms an unusual feature in the form of a series of inverted triangles. Finally the back pillar finishes just below the buttocks. This is unusual for Romano-Egyptian statuary, where the feature typically goes to the back of the head or mid-shoulder. On Egyptianising (and so classical) Roman statues the back pillar is absent.

No single model exists for these modern copies. The closest is a pair of black marble statues of Osiris-Antinous from Hadrian's Villa, now in the Egyptian Museum, Munich. Unlike the Fitzwilliam Museum copies, however, the Munich statues stride forwards onto alternate legs (Photograph). This characteristic was a Roman development; Egyptian statues always stride onto their left foot. The modern copies are also similar to two white marble Egyptianising statues of Osiris Antinous, also from Hadrian's Villa and now housed in the Vatican Museums. These statues were taken to Paris by Napoleon and returned to Rome at the end of the Napoleonic war (Poole 1986: 67). Like the Fitzwilliam copies the wrists of these essentially classical images are slightly up-turned and the feet are placed in a central position. It is also possible that the quarter length back pillar was intended to imitate the tree stumps at the back of the Vatican statues. The complete Vatican statue however shows Antinous with a *uraeus* (cobra) on his brow, whereas the Munich statues are without the divine cobra. The Fitzwilliam Museum's statues personify the close link between ancient and modern Egyptomania.

Rackham 1935: 909; Poole 1986: 67 no. J10.

Further reading: Grimm et al. 2003: 103-06; Ashton in McFarlane and Morgan eds. Forthcoming.

Coin references and abbreviations

BMC= R.S. Poole, *Catalogue of the coins of Alexandria and the Nomes*, London, 1892.

Dattari= G. Dattari, *Nummi Augg. Alexandrini*, Cairo, 1901.

Geissen=
A. Geissen, *Katalog Alexandrinischer Kaisermünzen der Sammlung des Instituts für Altertumskunde der Universität zu Köln, Band I, Augustus-Trajan (Nr. I-740)*, Opladen, 1974.

A. Geissen, *Katalog Alexandrinischer Kaisermünzen der Sammlung des Instituts für Altertumskunde der Universität zu Köln 3, Marc Aurel-Gallienus (Nr. 1995-3014)*, Opladen, 1982.

McClean= S.W. Grose, *Catalogue of the McClean Collection of Greek Coins 3, Asia Minor, Farther Asia, Egypt, Africa*, Cambridge, 1929.

Milne= J.G. Milne, *Catalogue of Alexandrian Coins*, Oxford, 1933.

RIC I= C.H.V. Sutherland, *Roman Imperial Coinage*, London, 1984.

RIC II= H. Mattingly, E.A. Sydenham, *The Roman Imperial Coinage*, London, 1926.

RPC I= A. Burnett, M. Amandry, P.P. Ripollès, *Roman Provincial Coinage I, From the death of Caesar to the death of Vitellius (44 BC-AD 69)*, London-Paris, 1992.

RPC II= A. Burnett, M. Amandry, I. Carradice, *Roman Provincial Coinage 2, From Vespasian to Domitian (AD 69-96)*, London-Paris, 1999.

SNG Lewis= I.A. Carradice, *Sylloge Nummorum Graecorum 6, The Lewis Collection in Corpus Christi College*, Cambridge. Part 2, The Greek Imperial Coins, Oxford-New York, 1992.

Bibliography and Further Reading

Albersmeier, S. 2002 *Untersuchungen zu den Frauenstatuen des Ptolemäischen Ägypten.* Mainz am Rhein: Verlag Philipp von Zabern.

Arnold, D. 1999 *Temples of the Last Pharaohs.* New York, Oxford University Press.

Ashton, S-A. 2000 'The Ptolemaic Influence on Egyptian Royal Statuary' in McDonald, A. and Riggs, C. eds. *Current Research in Egyptology.* Oxford: Archaeopress, 1-11.

Ashton, S-A. 2001 *Ptolemaic Royal Sculpture from Egypt. The interaction between Greek and Egyptian traditions.* Oxford: Archaeopress.

Ashton, S-A. 2002 'A question of authenticity of date?', *British Museum Studies in Ancient Egypt and Sudan,* Issue 2 February 2002. http://www.thebritishmuseum.ac.uk/egyptian/bmsaes

Ashton, S-A. 2003 *Petrie's Ptolemaic and Roman Memphis.* London: Institute of Archaeology, UCL.

Ashton, S-A. 2003b *The last queens of Egypt.* Great Britain: Pearson Education.

Ashton, S-A. 2003 'Cleopatra: goddess, ruler or regent?', in Walker, S. and Ashton, S-A. eds. *Cleopatra Reassessed.* London: British Museum Occasional Papers, 25-30.

Ashton, S-A. 2003 'The Ptolemaic royal image and the Egyptian tradition,' in Tait, W.J. ed. *Never had the like occurred: Egypt's view of its past.* London: University College London, 213-224.

Ashton, S-A. 2004 'Ptolemaic Alexandria and the Egyptian tradition', in Hirst, A. and Silk, M. eds. *Alexandria, Real and Imagined.* Aldershot: The Centre for Hellenic Studies King's College London, 15-43.

Ashton, S-A. forthcoming 2004 'Roman Uses and Abuses of Ptolemaic sculpture in Italy', in McFarlane, F. and Morgan, C. eds. *Festschrift essays for Geoffrey Waywell.* London: Institute of Classical Studies.

Ashton, S-A. forthcoming 2006 *Hadrian. Emperor and Pharaoh.* Great Britain: Pearson Education.

Bailey, D.M. 1988 *A catalogue of the lamps in the British Museum 3. Roman provincial lamps. London:* British Museum Press.

Belli Pasqua, R. 1995. *Sculture di età Romana in 'basalto'.* Rome: L'Erma di Bretschneider.

Bianchi, R.S. 1980 'Not the Isis Knot', *Bulletin of the Egyptological Seminar 2,* 9-31.

Bianchi, R.S. ed. 1988 *Cleopatra's Egypt: Age of the Ptolemies.* Brooklyn: The Brooklyn Museum.

Bianchi, R.S. 1988 'Pharaonic art in Ptolemaic Egypt', in R.S. Bianchi, ed., 55-80.

Bianchi, R.S. 1996 'Pharaonic Egyptian Elements in the Decorative Arts of Alexandria during the Hellenistic and Roman Periods', in Green, P. ed. *Alexandria and Alexandrianism* Malibu, 191-202.

Birley, A.R. 1997 *Hadrian the Restless Emperor.* London and New York, Routledge.

Boatwright, M.T. 2000 *Hadrian and the Cities of the Roman Empire.* Princeton and Oxford: Princeton University Press.

Bosse-Grifiths, K. 2001 'A Beset amulet from the Amarna period', in Gwyn Griffiths, J. ed. *Amarna studies and other selected papers.* Freiburg and G tingen: Univerit tverlag und Vandernhoeck und Ruprecht, 51-63.

Bothmer, B.V. 1960 *Egyptian Sculpture of the Late Period, 700 B.C. to A.D. 100.* New York: The Brooklyn Museum.

Botti, G. and Romanelli, P. 1951 *Le sculture del Museo Gregoriano Egizio.* Vatican City: Tipographia Poliglotta Vaticana.

Bowman, A. 1990 *Egypt after the Pharaohs.* Oxford: Oxford University Press.

Breccia, E., 1934 *Terrecotte figurate greche e greco-egizio del Museo di Alessandria.* Bergamo: Officine dell'Istituto italiano d'arti grafiche.

Brady, T.A. 1978. *Collected Essays: Sarapis and Isis.* Edited by C.F. Mullet. Chicago, repr.

Buhl, M-L. 1955 'Remarks on a group of late Egyptian faience vases', *Acta Archaeologica* 26, 188-197.

Castiglione, L. 1958 'La statue de culte hellénistique du Sarapieion d' Alexandrie', *Bulletin du Musée National Hongrois des Beaux-Arts* 12, 17-39.

Charles-Gaffiot, J. and Lavagne, H. eds. 1999 *Hadrien Trésors d'une villa impéiale*. Milan: Electa.
Clairmont, C.W. 1966 Die Bildnisse des Antinous. Rome: Bibliotheca Helvetica Romana 6.

Desroches-Noblecourt, C. 1999 'Hadrien a Philae', in Charles-Gaffiot, J. and Lavagne, H. *Hadrien trésors d'une villa impériale* Milan: Electa, 63-74.
Dunand, F. 1990 *Terres cuites gréco-romaines d'Egypte*. Paris: Réunion des musées nationaux.
Dunand, F. 1998 'Priest bearing an 'Osiris-Canopus' in his veiled hands', in Goddio, F. et al. Alexandria. *The submerged royal quarters*. London: Periplus, 189-194.
Égypte Romaine 1997 = Égypte Romaine. L'Autre Égypte. Musées de Marseille-Réunion des musées nationaux.
El Daly, O. 2003. 'Ancient Egypt in Medieval Arabic writings', in in Ucko, P. and Champion, T. eds. *The wisdom of Egypt. Changing visions through the ages*. London: University College London, 39-64.

Fischer, J. 1994 *Griechisch-Römische Terrakotten aus Ägypten*. Tübinger Studien 14 zur Archäologie und kunstgesichte. Berlin: Ernst Wasmuth Verlag Tuningen.
Fjeldhagen, M. 1995 *Graeco-Roman Terracottas from Egypt Ny Carlsberg Glyptotek*. Copenhagen: Ny Carlsberg Glyptotek.
Frankfurter, D. 1998 *Religion in Roman Egypt: assimilation and resistance*. Princeton: Princeton University Press.
Fraser, P.M. 1972 *Ptolemaic Alexandria*. 3 vols. Oxford: Oxford University Press.
Friedman, F.D. ed. 1998 *Gifts of the Nile, Ancient Egyptian Faience*. London: Thames and Hudson.

Glare, P.M. 1993 *The temples of Egypt: the impact of Rome*. University of Cambridge Ph.D. Dissertation.
Grimm, A. et al. 2003 *Winckelmann und Ägypten Die Wiederentdeckung der ägyptischen Kunst im 18. Jahrhundert*. Tübingen.
Grimm, G. 1972 'Two early imperial faience vessels from Egypt', *Miscellanea Wilbouriana* 1, 71-100.
Grimm, G. 1974 *Die Römischen Mumienmasken aus Ägypten*. Wiesbaden: Franz Steiner Verlag GMBH.

Harris, J.R. 1996 'Mithras at Hermopolis and Memphis', in Bailey, D.M. ed. *Archaeological research in Roman Egypt*. Ann Arbour: Journal of Roman Archaeology: 169-76.
Himmelmann, N. 1983 'Realistic Art in Alexandria', *Proceedings of the British Academy*, London 67, 193-207. Oxford: Oxford University Press.
Hölbl, G. 1984 'Serapis', *Lexikon der Ägyptologie* 5, 870-874.
Humbert, J-M. Pantazzi, M. and Ziegler, C. eds. 1994 *Egyptomania. L'Égypte dans l'art occidental 1730-1930*. Paris: Réunion des musées nationaux.

Kaczmarczyk, A and Hedges, R.E.M., 1983. *Ancient Egyptian Faience*. Warminster: Aris and Phillips.
Kiss, Z. 1984 *Études sur le portrait impérial Romain en Egypte*. Warsaw: Travaux du Centre d'Archéologie Mediterranéenne de l'Académie Polonaise des Sciences 23.
Krauss, R. 1980 'Isis' *Lexikon der Ägyptologie* 3, 186-203.

Lambert, R. 1997 *Beloved and God. The Story of Antinous and Hadrian*. London: Phoenix Giant.
Langton, N. 1940 *The Cat in Ancient Egypt, illustrated by the collection formed by N&B Langton*. Cambridge: Cambridge University Press. Reprinted in 2002 London: Kegan Paul
Lembke, K. 1994 *Das Iseum Campense in Rom: Studie über den Isiskult unter Domitian*. Heidelberg : Verlag Archäologie und Geschichte.

Lewis, N. 1970 '"Greco-Roman" Egypt, Fact or Fiction?' in Samuel, D.H. ed. *Proceedings of the Twelfth International Congress of Papyrology.* Toronto: American Studies in Papyrology 7, 1-14.

MacDonald, W.L. and Pinto, J.A. 1995 *Hadrian's Villa and its Legacy.* New Haven: Yale University Press

Malek, J. 1997. *The cat in Ancient Egypt.* Pennsylvania: University of Pennsylvania Press.

Malgouyres, P. 2003 *Porphyre La Pierre poupre des Ptolémées aux Bonaparte.* Paris: Réunion des musées nationaux.

Martin, G. forthcoming *A catalogue of stelae from ancient Egypt and Nubia in the Fitzwilliam Museum Cambridge.* Cambridge: Cambridge University Press

Maxfield, V and Peacock, D. 2001 *The Roman Imperial Quarries. Survey and Excavation at Mons Porphyrites 1994-1998. Volume I: Topography and quarries.* London: Egypt Exploration Society.

Meyboom, P.G.P. 1994 *The nile mosaic of Palestrina. Early evidence of Egyptian religion in Italy.* Leiden: Brill.

Meyer, H. 1991 *Antinoos.* Munich: Wilhelm Fink Verlag.

Müller, H.W. 1971 *Il culto di Iside nell'antica Benevento :catalogo delle sculture provenienti dai santuari egiziani dell'antica Benevento nel Museo del Sannio. Benevento.* Saggi e Studi del Museo del Sannio Biblioteca e Archivio Storico Provinciali di Benevento.

Mysliwiec, K and Szymanska, H. 1992 'Les terres cuites de Tell Atrib. Rapport préliminaire', *Chronique d'Égypte* 67, 112-132.

Nachtergael, G., 1995 'Chronique Terres cuites de l'Égypte gréco-romaine. À propos de quatre Catalogues recent', Chronique d'Égypte 139, 254-94.

Nenna, M-D. and Seif El-Din, M. 2000 *La vaiselle en faience d'époque gréco-romaine* IFAO Études alexandrine 4, Cairo: Institut Français de l'Archéologie

Parlasca, K. 1983 *'Griechisch-römische Steinschälchen aus Ägypten'* in Aegyptiaca Traverensia 2: 151-60.

Petrie, W.M.F. 1905 *Roman Ehnasya (Herakleopolis Magna)* 1904. Plates and Texts Supplementary to Ehnasya. A Special Extra Publication of the Egypt Exploration Fund. London: The Egypt Exploration Fund.

Petrie, W.M.F. 1911. The pottery kilns at Memphis, in E.B. Knobel, W.W. Midgley, J.G. Milne, M.A. Murray and W.M.F. *Petrie Historical Studies.* 34-37.

Petrie, W.M.F. 1911b *Roman Portraits and Memphis* London: British School of Archaeology in Egypt.

Philipp, H. 1972 *Terrakotten aus Ägypten im Ägyptischen Museum Berlin.* Berlin: Gebr. Mann Verlag.

Podvin, J-L. 2002 'Lampes isiaques sur la toile mondiale' in Bricault, L. ed. *Isis en Occident Actes du IIème colloque international sur les Études Isiaques.* Leiden: Brill, 243-248.

Podvin, J-L. 2002 'Les lampes isiaques hors d'Égypte' in Bricault, L. ed. *Isis en Occident Actes du IIème colloque international sur les Études Isiaques.* Leiden: Brill, 357-376.

Poole, J. 1986 *Plagiarism personified? European pottery and pottery figures.* Cambridge: The Fitzwilliam Museum.

Rackham, B. 1935. *Catalogue of the Glaisher Collection of pottery and porcelain in the Fitzwilliam Museum Cambridge I.* Cambridge: Cambridge University Press.

Raeder, J. 1983 *Die statuarische Ausstattung der Villa Hadriana bei Tivoli.* Frankfurt am Main and Bern: Peter Lang.

Rausch, M. ed. 1998 *La gloire d'Alexandrie.* Paris: Réunion des musées nationaux.

Rose, C.B. 1997 *Dynastic commemoration and imperial portraiture in the Julio-Claudian period.* Cambridge: Cambridge University Press.

Roullet, A. 1972 *The Egyptian and Egyptianising Monuments of Imperial Rome.* Leiden: Brill.

Rowe, A. 1946 *Discovery of the Famous Temple Enclosure of Serapis at Alexandria.* London.

Sayce, H.A. 1907 'Excavations at Gebel Silsila', *Annales du Service des Antiquités de l'Egypte* 8 1907, 95-105.

Schmidt, S. 2003 *Grabreliefs im Griechisch-Römischen Museum von Alexandria*, Abhandlungen des Deutschen Archäologschen Instituts Kairo, Ägyptologische Reihe 17, Berlin: Achet Verlag.

Sheurleer, R.L., 1974 'Quelques terres cuites Memphites', *Revue d' Égyptologie* 26, 83-99.

Smith, R.R.R. 1988 *Hellenistic royal portraits*. Oxford: Oxford University Press

Smith, R.R.R. 1991 *Hellenistic sculpture*. London: Thames and Hudson.

SNG= Carradice, I.A. 1992 *Sylloge Nummorum Graecorum 6. The Lewis Collection in Corpus Christi College Cambridge*. Part 2 The Greek Imperial Coins: Oxford: The British Academy.

Stambaugh, J.E. 1972 *Sarapis Under the Early Ptolemies*, EPRO 25. Leiden.

Stanwick, P.E. 2002 *Portraits of the Ptolemies. Greek kings as Egyptian pharaohs*. Texas: Texas University Press.

Stewart,A. 1993 *Faces of power. Alexander's image and Hellenistic politics*. Berekeley/Los Angeles/Oxford: University of California Press

Strudwick, N. and Strudwick, H. 1996 *The tombs of Amenhotep, Khnummose and Amenmose at Thebes*. Oxford: Griffiths Institute.

Szymanska, H. 'Tell Atrib excavations, 1998', *Polish Archaeology in the Mediterranean* 10, 71-76.

Szymanska, H. 'Tell Atrib excavations, 1999', *Polish Archaeology in the Mediterranean* 11, 72-82.

Szymanska, H. and Babraj, K. 2004 'Aus den Brennöfen von Athribis (Ägypten): neue Funde aus dem ptolemäischen Stadtviertel', in *Antike Welt* 2004 vol. 34.

Takács, S.A.1995 *Isis and Sarapis in the Roman World*. Leiden: Brill.

Thompson, D.B. 1973 *Ptolemaic Oinochoai and Portraits in Faience, Aspects of the Ruler-Cult*, Oxford: Oxford University Press.

Thompson, D.J. 1988 *Memphis under the Ptolemies*. Princeton: Princeton University Press.

Török, L. 1995 *Hellenistic and Roman Terracottas from Egypt*. Bibliotheca Archaologica 15 Monumenta Antiquitatas Extra Fines Hungariae Reperta 4. Rome: L'Erma.

Uhlenbrock, J.P. 1990 *The Coroplast's Art.* New York: Aristide D. Caratzas.

Vassilika, E. 1995 *Egyptian Art.* Cambridge: Cambridge University Press

Vassilika, E. 1998 *Greek and Roman Art. Cambridge: Cambridge University Press.*

Venit, M.S. 2002: 'Ancient Egyptomania: The 'Uses' of Egypt in Graeco-Roman Alexandria', *Leaving No Stones Unturned: Essays on the Ancient Near East and Egypt in Honor of Donald P. Hansen* Ehrenberg, E. ed. Winona Lake, IL: Eisenbrauns, 261-278.

Venit, M.S. 2002: *Monumental Tombs of Ancient Alexandria: The Theater of the Dead*. New York: Cambridge University Press.

Versluys, M-J. 2002 'Isis Capitolina and the Egyptian cults in late Republican Rome' in Bricault, L. ed. *Isis en Occident Actes du IIème colloque international sur les Études Isiaques*. Leiden: Brill, 421-448.

Versluys, M-J. 2002 *Aegyptiaca Romana. Nilotic scenes and the Roman views of Egypt*. Leiden: Brill.

Walker, S. and Higgs, P. eds. 2000 *Cleopatra. Regina D'Egitto*. Milan: Electa.

Walker, S. and Higgs, P. eds. 2001 *Cleopatra of Egypt from History to Myth*. London: BMP.

Walters, E.J. 2000 'Prominence of women in the cult of Isis in Roman Athens: funerary monuments from the agora excavations and Athens', in Bricault, L. ed. De Memphis à Rome. *Actes du Ier Colloque international sur les etudes isiaques, Poitiers-Futuroscope 8-10 avil 1999*. Brill: Leiden-Boston-Köln, 63-90.

Weber, W. 1907 *Untersuchungen zur Geschichte des Kaisers Hadrianus*. Leipzig: B.G. Teubner.

Westendorf, W. 1980 'Isis-Knoten' *Lexikon der Ägyptologie* 3: 204.

Ziegler, C. 1994 'D'une égyptomanie à l'autre: l'heritage de l'Antiquité romaine', in Humbert, J-M. Pantazzi, M. and Ziegler, C. eds. *Egyptomania. L'Égypte dans l'art occidental 1730-1930*. Paris: Réunion des musées nationaux.